THE ADVENTURE ADVANTAGE

BOYDELL GLOBAL PRODUCTIONS

THE
ADVENTURE
ADVANTAGE

A ROADMAP INTO UNCERTAINTY, THROUGH FEAR,
AND ONWARD TO YOUR HEROIC LIFE

MICHAEL J. BOYDELL

In Celebration of the Adventure Advantage

"Warmly engaging, refreshingly authentic. Look no further if you've lost the script and are ready to reauthor your life."

—ELLIOT S. WEISSBLUTH, FOUNDER OF HIGHTOWER ADVISORS, ENTREPRENEUR, RACONTEUR

"When existential questions meet existential opportunity, you want Mike in your corner."

—KIM WEINBERG, FOUNDER OF COACH IN MOTION, GEORGETOWN UNIVERSITY LEADERSHIP FACULTY, YPO GLOBAL FACILITATOR

"The winning formula for elite and everyday performers: in the arena, on the podium, and over a lifetime."

—DR. CHRIS KLACHAN, CHIROPRACTOR WITH THE NATIONAL BASKETBALL ASSOCIATION, NATIONAL HOCKEY LEAGUE, WOMEN'S TENNIS ASSOCIATION, AND THE UNITED STATES OLYMPIC COMMITTEE

"A voice for the essential humanity interwoven in our individual and collective stories—across time, culture, and gender."

—GULNAR VASWANI, CHIEF CULTURE OFFICER, GLOBAL DEI SPECIALIST, BOARD TRUSTEE, CEO AT AKSARA FOUNDATION, YPO GLOBAL FACILITATOR

"Every executive's secret weapon—I don't make major life or business decisions without first seeking Mike's input."

—JOHN WARRILLOW, PRESIDENT OF THE VALUE BUILDER SYSTEM, BESTSELLING AUTHOR OF *BUILT TO SELL*, KEYNOTE SPEAKER, AND PODCAST HOST

"Now is the time for employers to spark the spirit of adventure into their workforce and workplace—for everyone's advantage!"

—ANDRO DONOVAN, MCKINSEY & CO. LEADERSHIP AND TEAM SPECIALIST, AUTHOR, FOUNDER OF AD CONSULTING LTD., YPO AND EO GLOBAL FACILITATOR

"Real-world experience plus psychological acumen—just the right mix of 'heart and edge' to ignite lasting growth!"

—DR. JP PAWLIW-FRY, *NEW YORK TIMES* BESTSELLING AUTHOR OF *PERFORMING UNDER PRESSURE*, ADVISOR TO ELITE ATHLETES AND GLOBAL ORGANIZATIONS, PODCAST HOST

"Time and time again, Mike's presence accelerates our growth—across the organization, as a team, and with key leaders. It's truly empowering to realize that depth of broad-sweeping and lasting impact."

—DAVE SPROAT, CEO OF YOUNG INNOVATIONS, MEMBER OF YPO CHICAGO CHAPTER, AND BOARD DIRECTOR AND TRUSTEE

"Michael's wealth of insight and depth of lived experience help immensely when considering significant, less-than-obvious decisions in work and life."

—COURT CARRUTHERS, PRESIDENT AND CEO, TRICORBRAUN; FORMER DIRECTOR, US FOODS AND RYERSON STEEL

"If ever we needed more adventure in our boardrooms, backyards, and bedrooms, NOW is the time! One-on-one, in group retreats, or when guiding an entire audience of diverse professionals from around the world, Michael has a sixth sense for seeing and liberating the best in us all."

—VINCE CORSARO, GLOBAL LEADERSHIP DEVELOPMENT SPECIALIST, FELLOW ADVENTURER, YPO GLOBAL FACILITATOR

"This book offers a bold and kind way to write the story of your life. Witnessing his journey, I am in awe of Mike's courage to question his own narratives and ability to invite readers to take ownership of their lives."

—TRINE BLÜCHER, EXECUTIVE COACH, LICENSED MARRIAGE AND FAMILY PSYCHOTHERAPIST, NARRATIVE THERAPY SPECIALIST, YPO GLOBAL FACILITATOR

"With brilliant, soulful commitment to self-realization second to none, Mike guides those ready to live new dimensions of mind and body, heart and soul."

—MITCHEL GROTER, CEO AT QUANTUM ACHIEVEMENT GROUP,
CEO AND FAMILY OFFICE ADVISOR, YPO GLOBAL FACILITATOR

"Adventure tests what we're made of and leads to where we're meant to be. Michael Boydell lays this opportunity at our feet, inviting us to step 'out there,' at a time when we need freedom more than ever."

—KAREN BRODY, BESTSELLING AUTHOR OF *OPEN HER* AND #1 MAN COACH
TO THOUSANDS OF HAPPILY MARRIED MEN

"Mike helped me identify behaviors stifling my growth and channel my authentic strengths to help myself, my employees, and clients. His work is the breakthrough puzzle piece for those seeking the next best version of themselves."

—AYESHA ROLLINSON, FOUNDER AND TEAM LEAD AT TEAM ATOMICA,
FORMER PROFESSIONAL TRIATHLETE AND ELITE NATIONAL TRIATHLON TEAM MEMBER

"Before meeting Mike I had a big goal without a clear strategy. We shifted my leadership style and created a roadmap my whole team embraced. Within two years, my life reached new altitudes. Never has growth felt so attainable and liberating!"

—BERRY MEYEROWITZ, SEASONED MEDIA FOUNDER AND CEO AT PHASE 4 FILMS,
ENTERTAINMENT ONE, AND QUIVER DISTRIBUTION AND CAPITAL

"Claim your independence. Create prosperity with others. Level-up everlasting vitality. You are holding the key to your new life of adventure!"

—ALEX PETTES, RETIRED-CEO TURNED PILOT, AUTHOR, PHILANTHROPIST,
AND GLOBAL ADVENTURER

BOYDELL GLOBAL PRODUCTIONS

Copyright © 2023 Michael Boydell
All rights reserved.

THE ADVENTURE ADVANTAGE
A Roadmap into Uncertainty, through Fear, and Onward to Your Heroic Life

FIRST EDITION

ISBN: 978-1-5445-4141-9 *Hardcover*
978-1-5445-4142-6 *Paperback*
978-1-5445-4143-3 *Ebook*

To my sons Jackson and Troy.

How it fills my soul to witness your adventures.

To my father, Craig.

As we turn to respect, celebrate, and thank each other through the silent gift of timeless love—thumbs-up.

I'll see you around.

Clean Pass

Note the arc of my adventures, so far...
reap only that which frees you too.
Leave the rest to dust.

My fears and failings serve me well.
They are not yours by birthright or association.
They are not needing your attention or remedy.

My dreams and desires serve me well.
They are mine to pursue, realize, or release.
They warrant neither reverence nor replica.

My heart is a warm and open home.
Come as you are and unburden,
shelter, share, eat, and drink.
Rest, recover, renew, and
before daylight breaks, go
meet your day waiting.

Tend to the adventure inside you, now
as you would shepherd a child
through sun-kissed field,
babbling brook,
or stormy night.

Fly as high and effortless as tailwinds allow.
Draw from the wisdom of earth beneath each step.
Feed the flame of your own wildfire.
Reflect in the clarity of calm water pools.

Note the arc of your adventures, so far...
sow only that which frees you to
gift a clean pass.

—Michael Jess Boydell

Contents

Clean Pass xi

Wake-Up Call xv

In Retrospect, It Was a Painfully Confusing Time 1

PART 1
WELCOME TO BASECAMP!

CHAPTER 1
The Anatomy of Adventure 29

CHAPTER 2
The Arc of Adventure 45

CHAPTER 3
The Axes of Adventure 91

PART 2
THE THREE GREATEST ADVENTURES

CHAPTER 4
Welcome to the Freedom Adventure! 135

CHAPTER 5
Welcome to the Courage Adventure! 179

CHAPTER 6
Welcome to the Power Adventure! 227

PART 3
WELCOME BACK TO BASECAMP!

CHAPTER 7
How to Extract Real Meaning and Ensure Lasting Growth 307

CHAPTER 8
How to Traverse the Most Common Post-Adventure Pitfalls 317

Return Home 327

CHAPTER 9
In Retrospect, It Was All One Big Adventure 333

Acknowledgments 345

About the Author 349

Wake-Up Call

Can't sleep.
Must be morning by now.

Check my phone.
4:12 a.m.—WTF?!

Another round of that recurring nightmare.
Looping the same grainy, final scene. Like déjà vu
                                                         all
                                                              over
                                                                        again…

Shhh...
please don't wake my ego.
It really doesn't want you
to know this part.

Driving **hard**, pedal to the **metal**.
Struggling to summit the impossibly steep curve of a half pipe.
Escape ahead, but straight up.
Grasping for gas to **fight** against gravity,

the GRAVITY of it all...

a tidal wave *swelling*
overpowering my machinery
a final surge *tumbling*

upside down
downside up

landing alone in a truth shrouded in shadow
cut off, laid bare. In fear I am:

      Mentally: ~~spent~~
      Emotionally: numb
      Physically: **heavy**
      Spiritually: hollow

A desperate plea: *"what about me? does anyone see? will anyone care?"*

A harsh return: **"Enough whining! Really, WHAT IS YOUR FUCKING PROBLEM?"**

A quiet knowing, as suddenly I realize for myself a fresh breeze rising up...

a gentle whisper... a soulful invitation
to lay down the great burden...

"but wait! what if...?"

Spell shattered. Hope lost. Anchored in place.

Cut to fade...

Alarm at 6:15 a.m.

Snooze button. Times three.

Come on boy, shake off those demons.

Time to suit up and take on the same day again.

In Retrospect, It Was a Painfully Confusing Time

ON THE OUTSIDE, IT ALL LOOKED GOOD.

Pushing hard and driving fast for years. Doing what everyone expected. Abiding by the rules, like I was supposed to. Building the good things: family, home, career.

I had banked my first million early and was just getting warmed up. More money flowing easier than I'd ever imagined (*and was too young to comprehend*). The right house, on the right street, with access to the right schools. The right network. The right accolades. Feeling large, in-charge, and unstoppable.

Yet disruptive forces kept interrupting my perfect plans. The career move that should have been. Self-absorbed shareholders. People not falling in line. The meaning that money was supposed to bring. The death of dear friends in their prime—two to cancer, one shot and killed instantly. Life was beginning to feel random and senseless. Uncertainty became something to anticipate and overpower, or simply avoid, at all costs. My mind worked overtime to bury any sign of emotional turbulence and maintain the semblance of control.

> *At each invitation to slow down I chose*
> *instead to plough through.*

Some pretentious suit at a gala dinner asked what I'd learned from my biggest failure so far. Yeah, right. I replied with a wink: "You must have me confused with someone else. I'm the guy who never fails." (Cringe. Not the first time my ego blinded me from a genuine dose of wise, compassionate, and well-timed counsel.)

With every part of my life so perfectly compartmentalized into all the right allocations and percentages, there was simply no room for failure. Yet that same approach also left no daylight for life *to* happen. It was an ironic juxtaposition of self-sabotage: striving so hard to deny the gifts of human frailty.

To be clear, my world was abundant with timeless treasures of pure joy, shared accomplishment, and loving connection to the important things that really mattered in my family, parenting, personal, and working life.

But on the inside, a new battle was brewing:

An artist blocked from creative expression. A student starved for deeper learning. A wolf pulsing to run hot and wild. A tender heart longing to hold and be held. A lion wanting to roar.

As time marched on, preserving that unflappable pretense of flawless success left me depleted. All that invisible armor served only to guard my own imperfections, leaving me afraid to ask for help at the very time I needed it most. Uncertainty loomed large. Ghosts of self-doubt lured me down distracting detours, away from the better parts of my nature, pulling me into a swampland of fears that started showing up as:

- **F**rustration. Guarded and angry. Blaming a world that seemed to conspire against me.

- **E**nvy. Coveting, on the outside looking in. Anxiously and perpetually pleasing others.

- **A**voidance. Diverted and distracted. Doing anything to resist or escape the reality of my situation.

- **R**umination. Constantly critical. Flipping between past regrets and future fictions (that always ended badly).

Somewhere along the way, my line of sight had plunged in altitude and I could no longer see the big picture. I struggled to imagine inspiring ideas while staying focused on the facts clearly blipping on my radar. It was as if my navigation systems were tuned to only the urgent tasks two inches from my face. Days became governed by the relentless, rolling to-do list. I rushed around like a distracted juggler with a few too many balls in the air, at every turn finding another problem to fix or crisis to avert—as if it was all on me to shoulder, swoop in, and make things right again.

My attitude had become equally diminished. I'd stopped leading with my naturally bold and big heart, less able to hold compassion for others or tend to the turmoil growing inside myself. Consumed by playing *not to lose*, insensitive to the impact of my actions, I forgot what playing *to win* was all about.

Most alarming was how far I'd strayed from the essential plot of my own heroic life.

My former freedom was now ensnared in proving my worth by other people's definitions of whom I was *supposed* to be. My natural courage was caught up in chasing scarcity, as if it was my job to manipulate all the pieces on the board toward the ideal outcome only I could see. All the while, my true power was fading, misunderstood, and misplaced.

It took several painful reckonings before I finally answered that wake-up call and took ownership for the path my life was on. Tough stuff to tear apart, let alone admit openly:

- Curled up, heaving on a tiled bathroom floor of a five-star London hotel after an overly indulgent work dinner capped off by several-too-many swimming-pool-sized martinis. Rising to take a long look in the mirror. Facing the naked truth of shelving a lifetime dream to lead a work-live-play adventure in another country, just to evade the possibility of conflict or rejection.

- Ambushed (or so it felt) by a close circle of peers, whose bold compassion called bullshit on my polished, cunning attempts to explain away the unmistakable signs of a soul yearning for connection. Summoning the courage to step into the risk of voicing my deepest wants and dreams.

- Resigning as CEO after a frustrating year of losing myself in problems that were never mine to fix. Realizing my ego would go to any end to uphold the mirage of unblemished success.

- Digging in the dirt of long-buried yet unresolved childhood wounds. Confronting early lessons that shaped my formative identity to the meaning of work, money, family, and sex, subconsciously passed down by influential adults yet to tend to their own wounds inherited from generations past.

Under all the many layers, I knew it was time to get back in charge of the life I was designed to live.

With loving support, wise counsel, and dogged determination, I dug into my relationship with change and uncertainty. I learned to confront and befriend my fears, harness them, and grow beyond them. I reclaimed my independence and came to trust my freedom in its most authentic form. I reestablished joy in collaborating with courageous others to explore, create, and revel in new achievements, prospering beyond anything I was capable of on my own. I discovered ways to restore my vitality, tapping into the timeless and ample power sources already flowing in me, around me, and through me.

I started to see each moment of life, whether mundane, maddening, or magnificent, as one big adventure. An arc to travel, from one uncertainty to the next—while navigating fearful detours, making leap after leap into the unknown. I began to understand how best to lead with the essential abilities already baked into my design.

It wasn't a straight-line ascent, but eventually I found my way up and out of that impossibly steep curve of the half pipe. By applying an adventure outlook, I found my way back to the heroic life that had been patiently waiting for my return.

ENOUGH ABOUT MY STORY; WE ARE BOTH HERE FOR YOU

The finer points behind my cautionary tale don't really matter and are, of course, different from the particulars of your story. For now, let's use my story as our jumping-off point to get straight to the *real* stuff, stripped of pretense, bravado, or façade.

When we confront and share our real stories, something sparks for both storyteller and listener. What at first seems so different slowly fades to reveal the common story, the human story, and we see ourselves within it:

- We begin to reconnect with what's really going on, inside us, around us.

- We trust ourselves to shine light into topics and questions which may have been disregarded as inconsequential, unconnected, or possibly forbidding.

- We illuminate the meaning of fear to uncover what's been holding us back all this time.

- We begin to see the bigger, brighter version of life, and our places in it, in a way that fuels us forward.

Maybe you can relate. When you gift yourself a moment of quiet to consider the state of play in your own world of work, family, and romance, what stories come up for you?

- What topics or situations feel most uncertain? Notice any fears diverting your time and energy? Which ones feel most familiar: frustration, envy, anxiety, rumination?

- Has an unwelcome disruption crashed the big life party you'd planned? An untimely takeover, trade, or termination? A global pandemic or economic plunge? A diagnosis or betrayal? The loss of someone close?

- Does a more serious reckoning finally have you firmly in its crosshairs? The false promise of chasing the big payday? The real cost of tolerating toxic tension? The reality of some inconvenient truth you can no longer avoid?

- Are you on the verge of a more intentional transition? A career shift or whole new chapter? The end or beginning of an important relationship? A big move to upsize, downsize, or right size? Maybe a specific adventure is now calling to you.

- Are you feeling beholden or trapped, like an imposter in a life that deep down doesn't feel like your own?

- Having worked hard to claim your independence, are you now energized to join forces with others to create and prosper beyond anything you could accomplish on your own?

- Do you find yourself revisiting your relationship with work, wealth, health, family, sex…or the meaning of it all?

- When was the last time you had a break from it all? Just for you, just because.

Wherever your answers to such questions land, rest assured, you are not alone.

Over decades I've been invited to witness thousands of real stories—every form of life's ups and downs, trials, traumas, and triumphs imaginable—all by accomplished and aspiring individuals just like you. People from around the world, who take their work, love, family, and community commitments seriously. People driven to discover the best in themselves, for the betterment of the world around them.

The details of each individual story that appear so unique on the surface mask two common threads:

- The perpetual, sometime annoying, often painful challenge of confronting a life full of uncertainty and fear.

- The genuine desire to evolve and expand into the next, best version of living freely, courageously, and powerfully, but without the map or tools to know the way.

Problems arise for so many of us because we have become spectacularly skilled at directing our best energy outward—achieving, competing, creating, serving—while remaining equally *unskilled* at turning our best energy inward. That old saying about the shoemaker's children going barefoot is universally recognizable for a reason. Consumed with putting our "best foot forward," we are untrained in keeping our fear impulses at bay when (not if!) things don't go our way. Deep down, we realize that without inner course correction, the lives we most want, the ones meant solely for us, will remain just out of reach—forever elusive.

> *The ego naturally acts like a traffic cop on a loudspeaker: "Keep it moving, people! No imperfections, failures, self-doubt, or fears to see here!"*

Feeling some reluctance at first is completely natural. You want to keep the spotlight on *this* stuff to avoid having to acknowledge *that* stuff.

That's why I went first. To open a door for us to go through, individually, but never alone.

But you already sense all of this; otherwise, you wouldn't be holding this book. Something about the "same old same old" just isn't working. You've tried a bunch of things that didn't stick. Now you're ready to shake things up.

> *Good news: you arrived just in time.*
> *Life as you know it is about to change.*

When was the last time you let someone take you out for a coffee, a beer, or a walk with the offer to actually open up? To properly vent or just allow yourself to be seen, heard, and understood, with no judgment, no fixing, no other strings attached?

Well, that *is* happening, *right now*. I'm inviting you to make this all about you and the person you most want to be. In your chosen vocation and professional passions. In your family and most loving relationships. In your romance, when expressing tenderness and sharing your sexual fire. In your pursuit of the dreams that leave you feeling awake, alive, vital, connected, and relevant to the world around you.

The good part is, I'll bet you've tasted all of this before. You know *exactly* what you are after and the stakes involved.

Even better, nothing we are about to do requires adding anymore to your already full plate. In fact, being the person you were *designed* to be, and *most* want to be, enables you to shed loads of emotional weight and physical fatigue you have become accustomed to shouldering.

Better still, *that* person is precisely who the world wants you to be too. Your colleagues, customers, spouse, loved ones, friends, neighbors, and strangers you pass…heck, even your faithful dog or tabby cat. Quite literally, everything and everyone wins when you adventure into your heroic life of freedom, courage, and power.

HERE IS WHAT WE ARE GOING TO DO

At this point, you are probably wondering: what exactly *is* the Adventure Advantage, and how do I put it to maximum use in my life?

Let's start by asserting a basic belief.

> *Change is the constant and necessary catalyst for growth of all kinds.*

(If you know differently, please contact me directly and we will write *that* book!)

Apart from the sort of change one can predictably anticipate from birth to death over a lifetime, our world today is operating within a complex web of interconnected volatility far beyond what most of us are accustomed to, let alone comfortable with. For many, life feels like being in a state of perpetual permacrisis.

Beyond any tolerable dose of discomfort, our human wiring triggers inevitable fear/greed responses in one form or another. Our ability to listen, to take in any further information, becomes challenged. Our ability to perform at our best becomes severely compromised. Our views become polarized. Read the headlines. Observe your workplace. Talk with your kids. Go online. You know what I'm talking about.

The sheer breadth and depth of cumulative disruption is creating once-in-a-generation levels of uncertainty and fear and, for the adventurous, *opportunity*. When simple change or full-blown catastrophe comes knocking, the advantage goes to those who understand that:

- The quality of one's life is directly correlated to the quality of one's relationship with uncertainty and fear. Those two bedfellows are inextricably linked. They're part of the deal, and we don't get to exist in a world without them, pretend as we might.

- While uncertainty is by definition unpredictable, there is a predictable series of steps—a universal roadmap—that allows us to navigate our way *through* fear and arrive ready to show the best of ourselves where, when, and how it matters most (by consciously choosing to fear *less*).

- Everything you need is already inside you. The essential elements required to thrive in work, love, and play over a lifetime of adventure—vision, presence, empathy, and bravery—are hardwired into your design and accessible anytime, anywhere.

- A "heroic life" comes through taking on what I consider to be our three greatest adventures: freedom, courage, and power. Like a series of progressive growth challenges in ordered succession, each brilliantly prepares us for the next. As we evolve, so do our uncertainties and fears, and we find ourselves revisiting this circuit of adventure time and again, over a lifetime.

By applying this advantage across our day-to-day pursuits, we expand the growth possibility and *probability* for ourselves—and for others.

The same is true in our worlds of work, career, and professional pursuits. Consider for a moment the leadership traits in consistently high demand. What are the traits at the core of professional development and performance improvement programs, or simply the behaviors we admire most as colleagues, shareholders, or paying customers? (Hint: You don't need reams of research or scientific studies to accurately intuit an answer.)

Across situations and sectors, we revere those with the ability to:

- Be curious, spot opportunities, and champion a compelling path toward an inspiring future.

- Discern signal from noise; laser in on the facts, questions, or decisions that matter most; and direct resources to them.

- Foster diverse relationships forged in emotional connection, trust, and collaboration.

- Act in the face of risk and ambiguity with confidence, integrity, and boundary.

Adopting an adventure mindset in our work and workplaces hones each of these traits, paving the way to smarter, more prosperous organizations and institutions, healthier cultures and communities, improved performance among teams and groups, and deeper connections throughout the constellation of relationships we cherish most.

Get ready. We are about to embark on a journey that will leave you transformed.

We are going to reclaim your sense of adventure. We will embark on a metaphorical and literal practice of navigating uncertainty and disruption to ignite lasting growth in the areas of life that matter most to you.

We will use plain language that is universally recognizable and easy to comprehend.

We are going to repurpose your relationship with fear. We will enable you to be with fear, channel it, and move beyond it. Along the way we are going to tap into the real essence of your abilities to imagine fresh and inspiring ideas, create kind and compassionate connections, be present with what is most real, and take assertive actions and decisions in the face of the unknown.

We are going to remove barriers and restore trust in yourself. We will rediscover the person you already are uniquely qualified, naturally designed, and wickedly expert at being. We are going to invite, create, and thrive in relationships to create and enjoy lasting prosperity. We are going to step into levels of power you have yet to realize—physically, intellectually, and emotionally.

We are going to equip you with tools to succeed. You will emerge with the *roadmap and toolkit required for success over a lifetime*. Even when you stumble (and you will, as we all do), you will know how to dust yourself off and emerge better able to know, show, and grow the best parts of yourself.

In the end, you will arrive at the heroic life that has been patiently awaiting, able to operate with the altitude and attitude necessary to succeed in any adventure that comes your way.

(And as a bonus round for those who go the distance, I guarantee a healthy dose of laughter and mind-altering epiphanies along the way.)

HERE IS HOW WE ARE GOING TO DO THAT

Shortly after answering my own wake-up call, I orchestrated a summer sabbatical. Against the advice of nearly every executive recruiter and to the confusion (and concern) of all but a few close friends and family, I chose to exit the world of "corporate CEO for hire" and venture out on my own.

The first step entailed unlearning the old beliefs that had governed my operating system to that point. I poured myself into any book, article, or framework that heralded "best practices" on managing change in individuals, teams, and organizations. Most I found repetitive and regurgitated or too theoretical, published by academics or self-proclaimed experts clamoring for attention. I found precious little hands-on experience or sharing of fears, failures, and battle scars. None of it spoke to what I was going through.

It all started to click when I got back out in the world and shifted to experiential learning through less traditional sources. Trading in the sterile safety of a screen-filled home office, I became a human test subject for the kind of real-world discovery that comes only from adventure.

Before long I found myself enthralled in the company of artists, writers, scholars, inventors, athletes, scientists, pioneers, and trailblazers, across cultures and genres. All of these voices, from their own time period, on their own terms, had come to grips with the universal power of disruption as the necessary catalyst for growth. Each treasured the eternal dance of duality—between light and dark; the divine feminine and the divine masculine. Each understood the wonders and limits of one's own mental capacity, the role of fear, and the thrills that follow every leap into the unknown. Perhaps above all, they held profound regard for the cycle of birth, growth, death, and rebirth, and the precious impermanence of all life amidst the vast, fluid, and forward-moving ecosystem of all that was, all that is, and all that has yet to become.

I invested in learning from those willing and able to share the humility in their own lived experiences through stories, songs, writing, and works of art in a way that connected with mine. Yes, universally, change can be painful, agonizing, and heart-wrenching. Life is not fair. Endings are sad. Beginnings are as messy as they are necessary to remind us of our need to shed that which no longer serves our ability to evolve.

I dedicated myself to overhauling my own operating system, rebuilding my toolkit, and honing my craft. After what felt like enough self-analysis, learning, and development for ten lifetimes, I became comfortable "playing jazz"—going into any situation ready to creatively play within a foundation of knowledge, able to voice notes of genuine human connection with bold confidence and clarity.[1] I came to believe that the greatest gift to ourselves—and the world at large—is our capacity to step into uncertainty, confront the fears waiting, and adventure beyond the once safe and familiar. I was ready to embark on a new personal and professional path dedicated to discovering, experiencing, and sharing the sort of practices that lead to healthy, prosperous, and responsible living.

I am going to guide you through the same adventure methodology that has helped thousands of other aspiring and accomplished individuals in solo pursuits, families, forums, and teams and organizations around the world.

Consider Part 1 of this book your orientation. As with all good adventures, our journey begins at basecamp, which is our place to assemble, build affinity, and get outfitted. I have designed basecamp in three chapters so you can easily learn the basics and explore more of what piques your interest:

---

[1] I am delighted to share some of many inspiring people and source materials that shaped my life and influenced this book as part of the final Acknowledgements section. I invite you to explore the names and works referenced in whatever way best serves your adventures ahead.

- Chapter 1. In "The Anatomy of Adventure" I debunk common stereotypes and leave you with a clear definition of what adventure is (and is not) all about.

- Chapter 2. In "The Arc of Adventure" I break down the predictable path every adventure follows. You'll examine the roadmap of what to expect and how to keep yourself steadily progressing forward, from initial disruption to ultimate joy.

- Chapter 3. In "The Axes of Adventure" I reveal the four essential elements that come preloaded in our human design: vision, presence, empathy, and bravery. You'll learn how these elements are everything required to calibrate your altitude and attitude and succeed in a lifetime of adventure.

As we make our way through basecamp orientation, we pause for occasional "rest stops." These short breaks enable you to reflect and integrate key learning elements in manageable doses before moving on. Here you will find a few questions that invite you to personalize your orientation in a way that is most real, sensible, and suitable to your unique situation. Get yourself some form of adventure log book to take notes as we go, which will enhance both your retention rate and personal application.

After basecamp we depart for Part 2, where we embark on the three greatest adventures in their important order of natural succession:

- Chapter 4. In "Welcome to the Freedom Adventure!" you will come to know and trust your authentic independence, the prerequisite for all adventures that follow.

- Chapter 5. In "Welcome to the Courage Adventure!" you will step into the world of *inter*dependent relationships, by showing who you are and inviting, accepting, and thriving with others to create collective prosperity.

- Chapter 6. In "Welcome to the Power Adventure!" you will level up the sort of vitality that endures by growing who you are, embodying and celebrating the sanctity of all life.

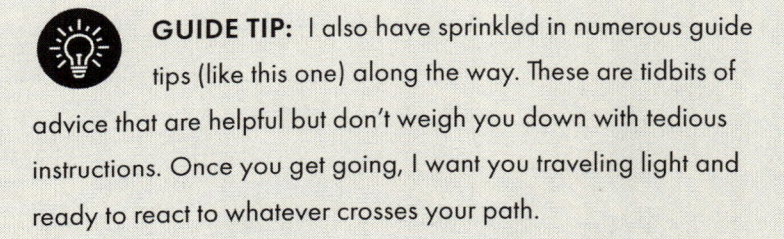

> **GUIDE TIP:** I also have sprinkled in numerous guide tips (like this one) along the way. These are tidbits of advice that are helpful but don't weigh you down with tedious instructions. Once you get going, I want you traveling light and ready to react to whatever crosses your path.

Each of these adventures follows a common flow so you can absorb the basics in manageable doses and build your understanding and application of new content along the way. Each adventure begins with:

- Details of the thrills that await and the risks of not completing what you start.

- A synopsis of what the adventure is all about.

- A trail guide of what to expect along with tips on how to keep advancing forward.

You are then offered a brief warm-up before taking on a series of built-in expeditions. Think of these as the progressive stages required to ascend to the summit of each adventure. This is where you get to create your own real-life adventures. You get to sample from the sort of winning activities others have benefitted from in large audience workshops, small group and team adventure retreats, and individualized programs. Your job is to proceed in whatever manner and pace feels right. Each adventure concludes with a "rite of passage"—a special opportunity to commend and celebrate your achievement so far.

Part 3 marks our return to basecamp, where we reassemble and you learn how to extract maximum value from your adventure experiences. From there we conclude with a final step-by-step summary of everything you need to thrive in your new life of adventure ahead.

FINAL DOUBTS, OR GO TIME?

All of us have been right where you are, *right now*. More than once.

That doesn't mean I pretend to know the intricacies of your situation. Like all of us, you got lost somewhere along the way, disoriented, or maybe completely adrift without a clue where to turn. Either way, you're ready to own your life again.

Pause for a moment to consider…that big obstacle, opportunity, or decision facing you now has been taking shape for *precisely the same number of years you have been alive*. That is a lot of time for habits to build.

So let's keep it real. Whatever you are facing is not going to be magically resolved in an hour, a day, or a week. And let's also agree that the only thing better than to have started way back when is to commit to starting right here, right now.

*My friend, adventure is not a spectator sport.
Ask yourself: if not now, when?*

I suspect that your world, like mine, is crowded with newsletters, clickbait, video posts, and parlor tricks all selling some kind of one-size-fits-all solutions, quick-hit prescription cures. So, this may come as a surprise, but I'll say to you what I tell everyone upon first meeting.

Don't take my word for it. Or anyone else's for that matter. When you encounter any big question, listen to *yourself*. That's the voice that matters most.

Yes, this book can be your guide, but we need to stop assuming the answers are somewhere beyond our own backyards. Everything you need is already in you, waiting to be discovered and ready to be released. Always has been. Always will be.

"The answer lies within" is not some bullshit, Zen-riddle mumbo jumbo. It's as simple and timeless a truth as you'll ever find. In fact, all of what I am offering to share has been true for centuries. These truths belong to all of us, across genders, cultures, ethnicities, time, and place. And you can bet those same truths will be around long after you and I are dust in the wind.

*This is your time to author what comes next.
And you hold the only pen that matters.*

What I know is that if you have what it took to get yourself to this point, to these pages, you have *exactly* the right ingredients to move yourself forward. Don't expect an immediate fast pass to that dream job, stress-free parenting, riches and retirement, rock-star sex, the love of your life, or a lasting purge from all your demons. While those outcomes (and more) are entirely within your reach, this book does ***not*** prescribe precisely where to go, what to do, how to get "there," or even when you'll arrive.

And be honest, would you let someone else wrestle away the steering wheel while on the ride of your life? Do you want someone else taking credit for your work? If that's your modus operandi, this book isn't for you. You'll make it partway through, give up, and be back adrift, searching for answers you'll never find. But who knows, maybe staying stuck in place is your destiny.

> *Here's the hard truth: if you're not ready for things to get uncomfortable, honestly, stop now.*

And, please, save your breath if you're still trying to convince yourself and anyone who will listen that change "just isn't your thing." Seriously, think about it. If that were true, you'd still be crawling around on all fours. But if that's where you land for now, that's okay. Come on back when you're ready. You'll know when. Your adventures will be right here, waiting.

If instead you're ready to stop being a tourist and take hold of the life you most want to inhabit, then consider this book your very own ready, willing, and able adventure companion. It will point you where you most need to go and be a beacon along the way. It might just become the most worn-in, dog-eared, scribbled-on book you'll ever own.

What awaits is your rightful place in a world of independent thinkers, honorable leaders, wise warriors, gifted artists, spirited dreamers, dark knights, and sensual lovers. Powerful company. All of the purest, noblest kind.

The road ahead is a complete game changer. Once you get the ball rolling, the right signs will start showing up. Powerful forces will arrive at just the right time, to cheer you on and pave the way. And not just for you, but for everyone in your life today and everyone who will follow.

This is not a drill.

Your evolution will not be televised.

Welcome to your wake-up call.

*Next stop: **basecamp**, where your adventure awaits.*

(Your move.)

PART 1

WELCOME TO BASECAMP!

Toss your bags. Grab a coffee. Find a chair. Join the circle.

From wherever you've come, whatever it took to get here, I'm thrilled you made it because it's a jungle out there. We're currently experiencing:

- A long-haul global pandemic, upheaval, isolation, exhaustion, and reinvention.

- Worldwide hostilities and political and economic volatility.

- Important, unresolved questions around social equality and systemic injustice.

- Dizzying technology advances polluted with disinformation.

- Continued climate change, pollution, and increasing harm to our global ecosystem.

- Dynamic shifts in the meaning of work and the workplace.

- More gun-related violence in our cities, schools, homes, and gathering places.

- Confusion over the meaning of feminine and masculine and the right to choose.

- Outright dysphoria and polarization from extremes on both sides.

(Add whatever you think we've missed on the big board.)

Our challenges are as real and complex as they are timeless and ubiquitous. It can be tempting to cut ties with the common human story that holds us together, to assume forces are conspiring against us personally, and to feel unfairly victimized. Finding safe and solid ground in so much uncertainty can be confusing, infuriating, and, at times, desperately lonely.

Amidst it all, I suspect you've arrived with notions of a bigger, brighter, bolder version of the person you most *want* to be and what just *might* be possible, for you and the world around you. I believe in that person too. I'll bet those closest to you believe as well, as do countless others you have yet to meet (but will soon enough).

Most people arrive at basecamp with a blend of cautious optimism and trepidation. As eager as you are to get this party started, your mind may be cycling through self-doubt and cynicism. Maybe you're ready to armor up at the first whiff of vulnerability or reject all talk of (gasp) "feelings." Or maybe you're ready to vomit at the opening verse of "Kumbaya."

Well, fellow adventurer, welcome to the club.

But fear not. Or more to the point, fear less.

Tune in to the wise, resonant, inner voice saying, "Relax. You are exactly where you are supposed to be. Trust you belong and were custom-made for this moment."

From now on, you are only as alone as you choose to be.

Remember, we are here to adventure. This is not yet another self-help book that offers a glimpse into the trials and tribulations of others without asking you to take accountability for your own work. I am not here to promise a quick-fix, five-step, one-size-fits-all program or find a sneaky way to coax you into therapy. Our goal is not mining for psychological pain. We won't be walking barefoot on burning coals, running wild and naked through a midnight forest, crafting bead bracelets, or chanting in a drum circle…at least not before lunch. (Cue nervous laughter.)

Mostly what we won't be doing is feeding fearful impulses:

- We will not vilify the alpha masculine or admonish the gentle feminine, nor shame how those noble traits flow within all genders.

- We will not indulge self-obsession or self-righteousness.

- We will not cancel our own ability to listen and learn by perpetuating overblown stereotypes, remaining silent on extremist sentiments, or writing revisionist history.

- We will not tolerate toxic behaviors that would seek to defuse the essential freedom, courage, and power in all human beings, in all sentient beings.

- We will not blame others when and where we get stuck.

(And if any of those agreements are getting stuck in your throat, you are definitely in the right place!)

Well, then, just what *will* we be doing?

The whole premise of answering the call to adventure aims to liberate the world of such negative, neutralizing, and polarizing ideas and the immeasurable suffering that results.

The adventures awaiting you hold endless downstream benefit to people everywhere. Of all social backgrounds. Of all origins and orientations. Of all ethnic and economic realities. Your adventure work, when done right, will pay immediate returns *and* recurring dividends to you, around you, and in everything that follows you.

> We will have fun discovering and laughing (at ourselves).
> We will get messy and wild. We will drop
> the armor, the masks, and get real.

We will dig into topics that typically don't see the light of day, dispel outdated beliefs, and discover seriously game-changing aha moments. Prepare to shatter the limits you may have concluded were irrevocably rooted in your life. Get ready to step into spirited, big-hearted, wise, and daring work. And for those who go the distance, the most awe-inspiring and life-awakening adventures await. Truly.

No doubt you will attract and meet other inspiring travelers on the same journey. In fact, I guarantee that as you progress, others will seek you out, magnetized to the strength of your emerging freedom, courage, and power with genuine admiration and respect.

They will want to learn from you.

They will want to build, create, and feel alive with you.

They will want to adventure with you.

Rushing is the ruin of real adventure.

As we get rolling, I want to share an important experience from a lifetime of working with all manner of folks driven to become more:

It's not only normal, but highly predictable that you'll want to speed through the basecamp orientation pages ahead.

Please don't. Or if you do, don't be surprised when some brilliant epiphany quickly fades into nothingness and you're left with an experience void of any lasting meaning. Your basecamp orientation has been laid out in bite-sized doses. I provide what you need at a pace that is absorbable, relatable, and transferable so you can build a foundation for what comes next.

Take your time with these sections. I promise you won't *unlearn* anything.

Before we proceed, I want to share a final tip I've learned the hard way, from personal experience:

Give your ego polite (yet firm) instruction to take a long walk while we get to our adventure work.

Otherwise, your old beliefs (aka self-indulgent, self-imposed limitations and fear stories) are going to keep hijacking the real adventures you're meant to discover. The necessary endings, the barren in-between plateaus, the messy middle, the fragile seeds of organic beginnings. The strong roots and soaring triumphs that follow.

Let go of everything you *think* you know, especially the stuff you think you know *for sure*, and trust in the adventure ahead.

CHAPTER 1

The Anatomy of Adventure

Technology advances that promise efficiency but require always-on access…the allure of instant gratification and false sense of control…endless online image management and self-promotion driving a heightened sense of FOMO (fear of missing out). Such forces combine to conspire against the real meaning of adventure.

Too often, we set unrealistic "adventure" expectations by throwing gobs of money and precious time chasing glittering prizes awash with endless compromises. Off-the-shelf travel packages. Canned scenic tours. Staged wilderness expeditions. Deep down, we crave more.

This is our time to think, feel, act, and live beyond bucket lists; tired metaphors; outdated imagery; systemic cultural, racial, and gender bias; and social stereotypes found in the typical modern-day lexicon, such as:

The lean, grizzled climber, typically male, even more typically white, suited up in thousands of dollars of gear gazing toward a snowcapped peak.

That might work for a small portion of the population, during a small percentage of time. But we are on the hunt for the sort of adventure that lives and breathes on your average Tuesday afternoon. Whether by design or in response, your work—our work—is all about embarking on the sort of real adventures that answer the call inside you. Anytime. Anywhere.

So often we find ourselves at the doorstep of adventure without realizing we've arrived. Commercial stereotypes have robbed us of the true Anatomy of Adventure.

We're stealing it back.

• • •

HOW WE (RE)DEFINE ADVENTURE (HINT: IT'S AN INSIDE JOB)

A quick look into the etymology of the word *adventure* is the perfect place to start:

- *Ad venire*: to come to, reach, or arrive at
- *Adventura*: a thing about to happen; to dare, take risk, face loss
- *Aventure*: chance, fortuitous, fortune

For our purposes, the Anatomy of Adventure begins by simply *arriving* at that time and place when "what's next" is about to happen, at work, at home, or wherever we happen to be.

But it's not enough just to arrive. Paying attention is critical. We have to see it and know it in order to be fully tuned in to those moments of divine design or happenstance. Otherwise, we miss the call of those seemingly random, accidental events, mammoth or mundane, that contain something fortuitous, meant just for us. An epiphany. A chapter to close. A door to open and step through. Amidst the vast sea of opportunity, adventure is about the waves we catch in fleeting moments.

But what's at risk if we refuse to answer the call or stray too long from adventure?

THE SUFFERING WE ENDURE

A certain amount of suffering is simply part of living a full life. True love comes with heartache. No risk, no reward. Think of joy and pain as opposing sides of the same coin, eternally in our pocket. We can pull it out anytime. Flip it to whatever side we wish. But we can't have one without the other.

But if we feel insecure in our own skins, or alone in our own company, we never come to trust the call to adventure. That's the kind of suffering that endures.

The immediate cost is to ourselves. We become numb to life. We deprioritize self-care. We devalue our freedom, courage, and power. We are left wandering aimlessly like a playlist on shuffle, like being stuck in a maddening loop of a single song on infinite repeat. As time wears on, the best of who we are is left to slowly wither away.

Gentlemen in particular: your attention, please. Check the insurance tables for the all-too-common checklist of a life in sharp decline: depression, waning physical health, poor sleep, low vitality, and denial of simple pleasures and personal hobbies. Poor time management, always on, 24/7 urgency. Little time invested in enjoying friendships. Low creativity, sexual fulfillment, or intimate connections. All clear warning signs of a reckoning on the horizon, at extraordinary personal cost.

THE RELATIONSHIPS WE LEAVE IN OUR WAKE

Our relationships suffer too. With a spouse or romantic partner, our children, extended family and friends, work peers, and the community. As we model and manifest internal suffering, those around us lose access to the best we have to offer. An inability to trust our own nature sends a clear, cautionary signal of our lack of trustworthiness to others. Pessimism, heavy energy, lack of substance, or volatile unpredictability become draining forces best bypassed and left behind.

AND THEN THE IMMEASURABLE COST TO THE LARGER WORLD

Losing touch with our own freedom, courage, and power means depriving the world of our most unique skills, professional contributions, and personal passions. We spend our prime years deferring to the dreams and priorities of others, chasing or living someone else's version of our lives. We become hooked on status, accumulation, and affirmation. Beholden to money. Locked into a life we never intended.

Predictably, sadly, and tragically, our children watch and learn. Every bit of what we're unable or unwilling to overcome gets passed down the line. A far cry from the family legacy we would feel proud to bestow and are actually capable of gifting generations that follow.

*This book you're holding is an adventure.
You've arrived at what's about to happen.
Pay attention—what's the call
waiting for your answer?*

Having realized the arrival at adventure's doorstep, our definition shifts to answering the call. Doing so comes with risk. To get the prize awaiting, we must pay a price. We have to give up something; more accurately, some part of us. Some belief or story we've been telling and retelling. Some unspoken, self-appointed role or subconscious motivation we've committed to for years, or for decades.

I want you to trust yourself with that risk of letting go. Trust in your ability to traverse whatever happens next. Trust that by staying the course, you'll ultimately arrive at a prize waiting just for you. Expect to feel disrupted (more on that ahead); consciously stepping into that disturbance is important and necessary. In the end, our Anatomy of Adventure looks like this:

I choose to see each new disruption as a personally fortuitous moment— an invitation to grow beyond and into unknown thrills waiting ahead.

(You might try saying that aloud a couple times to explore what comes up for you.)

With that definition in hand, we are ready to debunk the most common adventure myths. After that we will take our first rest stop, where you can personalize the theory and spark your own adventure engines.

Let's get started.

DEBUNKING COMMON ADVENTURE MYTHS

Our societal definition of adventure has become increasingly commercialized. Many of our idealized adventure ideas hold real promise but too often become watered down in the actual execution. Here are my Top 5 Adventure Myths contrasted against what the true Anatomy of Adventure is all about and the breakthroughs waiting for you.

Adventure Myth #1: Adventure must be expensive and elaborate.

You don't have to buy a bunch of costly gear and commit to seven years in Tibet. Sure, adventure can absolutely include exotic expeditions and grand solo treks; but it's by no means a requirement.

The Truth: Adventure surrounds you. Always. Patiently, persistently inviting you in, through and beyond.

Adventure starts with slowing down. Embracing open, still space, where the *being* takes precedent over the *doing*. The trick is maintaining momentum by seeing the mini adventure everywhere in day-to-day life. By finding the marvel in the mundane.

With practice, discoveries will flow together, each informing the next, as if by design. What might have seemed like a mystical epiphany or random coincidence will become regular occurrence. Soon, bigger and bigger adventures will reveal themselves and invite you in, a factor of staying open and awake to the possibility of adventure right in front of you. (And you won't believe how effortless this all works until you experience it firsthand.)

Whether your destination is near or far, pack as lightly as possible. Extra gear and baggage will only bog you down. Consider leaving your camera behind, so as not to miss or distort the essence of what you will encounter. Instead, take the photo with your eyes. Share the story from your soul.

> **GUIDE TIP:** Free and simple adventures can be part of any busy schedule. A phone-free day. A full-moon hike. A morning of uninterrupted creative output. An hour of communicating only with body language. A slow, observational walk along a stream or through a crowd.
>
> Explore genealogy, customs, and culture. Ask your kids to teach you something. Visit a library or museum. Invite your partner to spontaneous romance or risqué play.
>
> Journal your dreams. Eat and meet outside. Have a *real* offsite. Declutter. Unsubscribe.
>
> Or...embark on whatever adventure is calling to you most!

Adventure Myth #2: Adventures require struggle.

Many of us have experienced hardship firsthand or were indoctrinated with family stories where protracted suffering was equated with honor, even righteousness. When attempting to play this out in adult life, we can be prone to approaching adventure with an undercurrent of atonement. Or we simply feel bad about making time for the things that leave us feeling truly alive and unburdened.

Adventure is not about half measures, how much pain can be endured, or penance for some past transgression.

The Truth: Adventure is about discovering what's most worth living for, right here, right now, and can be simple and straightforward.

Yes, adventures often involve challenge, sustained grit, even grueling effort. But the real anguish and inner demons come from holding back from the truth inside you. Exorcising those ghosts as we adventure, even temporarily, immediately lightens the load.

> **GUIDE TIP:** Imagine the euphoric relief that comes with removing a deep splinter. It's the same when you finally grant yourself permission to live the adventure inside you. Try taking the long way home every day for a week and see what happens. Adventure can feel as effortless as merrily rowing downstream.

Adventure Myth #3: Adventures are dangerous, verging on reckless.

Yes, adventure requires putting some part of ourselves at risk. Nothing ventured, nothing gained. But at no point does adventure require risking physical safety, emotional security, mental health, or well-being—yours or anyone else's.

Those caught in that feeling of imposter syndrome might go to endless lengths to prove how extraordinary, invulnerable, and all-powerful they are. (If that sounds familiar, take note.) Rash decisions often result when we start competing *against* versus *with* formidable opponents, or when we plunge heedlessly to overpower forces of nature. This way folly, and danger, lies.

The Truth: Adventure is about living at your own continually expanding edge while respecting physical and psychological safety.

Yes, challenge yourself. But train properly, pack adequately, and lead with humility. Don't drag anyone else along unwittingly or invite unnecessary risk by trying to fill an emotional void that has no bottom.

At all times, adventure calls for the healthy respect of life and death and the impermanence in all things. It starts by approaching and befriending the deepest, sometimes darkest aspects of who we are. That means stepping to the edge of your *inner* brink, where fear and resolve are held together, without becoming overwhelmed. Sometimes adventure is simply knowing that *now* is the time for that difficult conversation or important step you've been putting off.

For classic type A incessant high-achievers (current or recovering), the real risk often lies in releasing attachments to external recognition, material gain, or expected outcomes. Letting go of historical identifications with self-worth—rooted in career, family, or parenting roles; in what it means to have money, be athletic, look sexy, or feel independent—may feel incredibly destabilizing. Adventure invites the continual redefinition of "Who am I now?" across our many roles and responsibilities in order to keep growing in sync with the big wheel of life.

> **GUIDE TIP:** Let that sink in. What identity attachments do you hold? How do you define self-worth? What do you want from others and why do you expect the world to work a certain way? Hint: Start by delving into how you identify with the big three—work, money, and sex—by considering these questions:
>
> - What roles and responsibilities do you hold for each?
>
> - Which of those are you gripping tightly, perhaps in defense of an outdated sense of self-importance?

> - Which are you holding loosely, perhaps ready to release in order to make room for renewed self-discovery?

Adventure Myth #4: Adventure is about achieving the next splashy "notch on your belt."

Glossy advertisements can be tempting: "Experience Africa's Big Five from the comfort of a luxury jeep and private 5-star accommodation!" Commercialized adventures promise all the rewards but negotiate out all the spontaneity. Beyond the plaques and high-adrenaline photos for the ego wall (physical or virtual), such adventures may have little lasting impact. Part of you may be satisfied, while another part is left empty.

Of course the big trip can be fun and worthwhile for you and your family. But throwing around big time, money, and energy does not guarantee an adventure. You may be setting yourself up to scratch only the surface and miss the experience *within* the experience, which is always where the real thrill lies waiting.

Ask yourself, what's the story you'd rather hear: the chest-pounding list of triumphs and depictions of how impressive and shiny my trophies are? Or my "you-can't-make-this-shit-up!" stories of plans gone haywire, pure comedic failures, near tragedies, gritty resolve, and heartfelt humanity that happened along the way?

The Truth: Adventure starts when discomfort kicks in.

Finally, the big trip. Exciting sights and sounds. Foreign languages. Jetlagged with daylight fading fast. Whoops. Lost luggage. Stolen ID and credit cards. Dead phone. Expectations shattered, right out of the gate.

When external forces dump a bucket of ice water on your perfect plan… when inconvenience or full-blown crisis comes knocking to wreak havoc on your job, sex life, vacation, education, finances, retirement, or entire life plan…now *you*'ve got yourself an adventure!

The best breakthroughs (best memories and best stories) follow the big breakdowns. Always.

> **GUIDE TIP:** May we agree, in the grand scheme of things, to not take ourselves so seriously? Let go of the idea that this book and the adventures you'll embark on are more "should" or "supposed to" or "have to" tasks to complete, more awards to acquire. Adventure is about getting out there, testing, trying, failing (yes, failing), learning, and living your life to the fullest.
>
> Maybe your next adventure is to create a "to-don't" list. Or better yet, a "fucket list."

Adventure Myth #5: Adventures are all about group getaways.

To be clear, I'm a big fan of offsites and retreats with colleagues, friends, and family. But the wine tastings, golf trips, road trips, and reunions offer different rewards than personal adventure: a change of scenery and pace, connectivity and camaraderie, levity and laughter, support and bonding.

And yes, of course, having a real adventure on these types of outings is possible. You'll just have to start in a place totally unfamiliar to anyone in your group and be 100 percent committed to breaking from the herd the moment your own call of adventure rises, at every point along the way. And believe me, it will!

The Truth: Adventure begins with a solo intention.

Adventure is about meeting what's most real in your life, right here, right now. That's going to be highly situational and unique from one person to the next. You might crave intellectual stimulation, while I want an outlet for creative expression. One person might be driven to physical challenge, while another desires a spiritual soul awakening.

Hold tightly to the clarity of your intention and hold loosely any master plan. Do that, and you'll land squarely in the adventure meant for you.

> **GUIDE TIP:** The point is to invest in your own adventures. If that feels uncomfortable, pay attention to what you're telling yourself. What inner narrative is getting in your way? If you have a friend with a similar adventure intention, agree to start and end together. Or start solo and link with people you don't yet know, or join forces with who (and what) you discover along the way.

* * *

REST STOP

This is a good time for a short break. Take a few deep breaths.

Let's take a minute to compare your preexisting adventure notions with the way adventure was defined in basecamp orientation. Sift through the ideas worth taking forward versus the ones best left behind. The best way to make that distinction is to apply what you're learning to the specific context of your own life today. How would you answer the following?

- When you think "adventure," what classic images or portrayals come up for you?

- With the benefit of hindsight, when in your past did an adventure arrive at your doorstep without you fully realizing it?

- Was there a moment when you arrived at an adventure opportunity but, at the moment of truth, hesitated or backed away entirely? What was the risk you chose to avoid? Was there a price you were unwilling to pay?

- Which of the Top 5 Adventure Myths have lured you in? Which adventure truths feel most real and relevant to who you are and who you're becoming?

- With your new understanding of the Anatomy of Adventure, when was your last adventure? When is your next one? Is there any reason why "right now" isn't the perfect time?

* * *

WRAP-UP

Personally, my best adventures have coincided with a meaningful bump or full-on jump in life trajectory. Some I stumbled upon, others I initiated. Each adventure experience left a unique impression—a lasting residue or ripple, creating fresh frequencies to tune in to and new waves to ride, thereby forever altering the course of what was to follow. A few personal favorites include:

- **Disenchanted college senior.** Choosing to pack my possessions and head west. Buying a one-way ticket. First real job, boss, and paycheck. First car (a used Toyota GTS, red, of course). First heartbreak.

- **Curious learner.** Signing up solo for classes and workshops to expand my comfort zone: Latin dancing, pencil sketching, total immersion swimming, Taoist breathing and sexual energy flow.

- **Pandemic pandemonium.** Stepping into personal fears during the early months of the global pandemic: isolation, financial losses, scarcity. Making intentional space to feel loss and grief. Shifting gears from waiting to creating. Discovering new ways to engage with virtual work. Expressing my voice through writing and art. Enjoying time alone.

Bottom line: adventure is all about those fortuitous moments, big and small, that surround us and wait patiently for our arrival. Through adventure we grant ourselves permission to go after those things most worth living for, to experience the fullness of what life is offering, in this time, in this place. Adventure invites a deeper conversation within ourselves, about how we relate to the world we inhabit.

Adventure is dynamic and comes with a free,
platinum lifetime membership:
choose it or lose it.

Whatever you choose, now is the time to punch your ticket and get aboard the life inviting you. Only you know the adventures calling and what is possible in your life.

ONWARD!

Now that you appreciate how the Anatomy of Adventure is an inside job, we can move on to the Arc of Adventure. There we will learn how to track the predictable path every adventure follows. I will point out the obstacles to anticipate and equip you with the tools to keep moving forward.

CHAPTER 2

The Arc of Adventure

Ahh, those rare moments when everything just "works." When life is in balance, with all engines aligned and humming, flowing between various roles and responsibilities with ease. That place of full and harmonious being, when past, present, and future blend and time itself stands still. You emit calm confidence with near celestial clarity, trusting yourself to be in sync with forces around you, as if by some thrilling and otherworldly design.

Such moments are the true prizes of life and are sweet to recall:

- Hitting full stride on a big project.

- Competing while "in the zone."

- Savoring the honeymoon phase in any relationship.

- Speechless, in awe of a surprise outcome, against all odds.

- An epiphany drop.

- Witnessing a beautiful birth or noble death.
- Swept away by a piece of music or loving embrace.

For however long the moment lasts—weeks, days, seconds—it won't go on forever. No matter how hard we worked to get there, how much we want to believe we "deserve" it, or how desperate our attempts to freeze time, we are guaranteed of one thing: the return of change, in some disruptive form, to spark our attention to the next new reality:

- Untimely news.
- A market swing.
- The exception (or modification) to the rule.
- The sound of the buzzer.
- The kids leaving.
- The death of a pet.
- Your partner's ideas that challenge your own.

What follows is the Arc of Adventure—your personal storyline of how you adapt (or resist) and how you grow (or shrink) in reaction to the disruptive uncertainties that shake your sense of normal. It is composed of predictable steps, a series of doorways to arrive at, enter, and move through in linear succession. None is more or less important. Each is valuable and necessary to ensure you continue to evolve as the world evolves around you. How cleanly you move from one step to the next versus how much you drag your feet is entirely up to you.

As toddlers and teens, we moved along this adventure arc with relative ease. In fact, our survival on the way to young adulthood depended on it. We were all born captive to imperfect parents. Cast into roles governed by spoken and unspoken family beliefs. Thrust into education systems that did or did not work. Bombarded with perplexing social influences. With no script, coach, or guide book, we just got on with it by utilizing our essential adventure abilities (more on those in Chapter 3).

Problems arise when we start trying to control more than we actually can—the "rules," an outcome, how another should think, feel, or act—and when we start feeling there is something big at risk of losing—our accumulations, our reputations and relationships, our sense of safety and security. We start playing small, tightly, and constrained. Self-doubt weighs down each step on the adventure arc. We get mired in the mess and force short-term fixes that subvert real progress. With wheels spinning (or while just plain stuck in the mud), we stand at the brink, unable to choose how best to move forward.

By illuminating each step along the way, using straightforward names, universal imagery, clear descriptions of what to expect, and tips on how to keep moving forward, we create a roadmap. It guides our way into uncertainty, through fear, and onward to the joys patiently awaiting our arrival.

Let's trace the Arc of Adventure with a short and simple example.

Suppose I was eagerly anticipating the prize of a long-awaited celebration dinner at my favorite restaurant, every detail meticulously planned. Upon arriving at the restaurant, there is no record of the reservation, no tables available. A disruptive change has just landed to create uncertainty as to how the rest of the evening will play out. We call this the *spark*. And just like that, my adventure has begun!

With expectations in disarray and no immediate solution, various emotional reactions—mine, my companions', the restaurant staff's—start to swirl:

Anger, blame, defensiveness…curiosity, hope, optimism.

This state of flux is the first step into the Arc of Adventure, aptly named the **mess.**

My brain (like all brains) is hard-wired to avoid or escape anything it deems "too messy." In nanoseconds, I am motivated to protect *my* version of the evening that was *supposed* to happen:

"Your records must be wrong…I see an open table in the corner."

My initial grasp to restore order (again, according to *my* definition) is the second step into the Arc of Adventure, which we call the ***fix.***

How much energy I commit to fixating on my past mental narrative (imposing my will to fight change) is completely up to me. But sooner or later, like it or not, consciously or subconsciously, I will arrive at an inflection point.

I can ignore, resist, or fight this new reality, stubbornly sticking to my version of how the evening was supposed to unfold:

"This is your problem. We're not going anywhere. I demand to see your superior!"

Or I can shift, adapt, and reset my orientation toward the reality of an uncertain future and move toward exploring a new version of how the evening *might* unfold:

"Any chance we could eat at the bar overlooking the kitchen? Do you offer takeout? Would you be willing to explore other options?"

That opening to shift from what was known to what is *not yet* known is the third step, which we refer to as the **choice**.

Uncertainty in all forms activates nervous tension between the many ways I imagine the story is destined to end badly (driven by my fears) and the many ways I imagine the story is destined to end well (driven by my ability to *override* those same fears).

If I stay fixed in the former, we can imagine how the story might end:

The celebration sours. Tensions boil over. Threats are exchanged. We bottle up the storm cloud on the ride home thus guaranteeing an equally tumultuous night.

This negative ending gets absorbed, shared, and passed on down the line—by me, the restaurant staff, and all onlookers.

If, instead, I am able and willing to choose the latter and move myself forward amidst uncertainty, before long I'll arrive at the final step of the Adventure Arc—you guessed it: the **prize**. This is where the entire scene, along with everyone in it, is transformed to a whole new reality, where everything aligns with effortless momentum.

We can imagine how that story might end:

A private table appears with a complimentary bottle from the owner. Delightful rounds of off-menu chef creations are enjoyed by all. Staff members share stories and first names are exchanged. An extra generous tip caps off a magical evening.

This positive ending gets absorbed, shared, and passed on down the line —by me, the restaurant staff, and all onlookers.

The pages ahead will orient you to the steps on the Arc of Adventure, each ending with a short rest stop so we can absorb and contextualize the critical takeaways before moving on. I'll conclude with a short overview highlighted with a few practical examples.

Off we go.

• • •

THE SPARK

The ground zero of every adventure. When disruptive change comes calling, small or significant, by random chance or intentional design.

> The spark icon blends several universally recognizable symbols of change: a lightning bolt, a starburst, an explosion. The edges are sharp and uneven, making it provocative to look at and slightly unnerving to approach or hold. The orientation on the longer spikes evokes a sense of accelerated movement toward the top right, up and out.
>
> The shape is neutral and open in the middle, inviting our own personalized caption:
>
> "POW!" "WHAM!" "WTF?" "YES!" "Nooooooo!!"

Change—or any kind of disruptive spark—is the constant, normal, and necessary catalyst for growth of all kinds. Given that we humans are ultimately defined by that which we are able to grow beyond (or not), the quality of your life starts and stops with how you relate to the spark.

The spark serves as an early detection signal of an adventure about to unfold. Failing to acknowledge the arrival or inevitability of the spark is what trips up (or completely blows up) our assumptions, expectations, beliefs, and best-laid plans. But sparks play an essential role in our development. They keep us humble, compassionate, sharp, and resourceful. They keep us tuned inward and outward, growing with what is most real and relevant in our here and now.

Seeing the sparks that invite adventure in the mundane of everyday life (technology glitches, rescheduled meetings, mood swings) is what prepares us for arrival of more disruptive sparks that invariably come calling at one time or another—the complete game changers, the blindsiding sucker punches (job losses, medical diagnoses, relationship issues). Learning to leverage the spark as a catalyst to our own growth is an essential adventure "muscle" to activate and strengthen over time.

> *Those deaf to the adventure call*
> *complain about change happening **to** them.*
> *Adventurers appreciate the change*
> *happening around them, **for** them.*

Here are the big takeaways of what to expect, with some tips on how to keep yourself moving forward.

The spark is really any change, event, or idea. Tiny or huge. In or out of your control.

Disruptive change may reveal itself slowly, over time, making the spark difficult to perceive. We barely notice each spring day gradually getting longer or the slow return of winter. We might overlook a hint of increase in signal noise or decay in communication. So too our measured migration from parental dependence to adult independence, and eventual return to requiring care from others.

The spark may be quiet, subtle, and easy to miss, like a new ingredient dropped into an old recipe. Something familiar now feels foreign. The once predictable is somehow less so. Like a door that has become sticky to your key. A crack of light from a usually dark passage. A whispered request from an otherwise silent voice.

Conversely, the spark may crash through the front door, commanding your attention, impossible to avoid. A shocking betrayal or sudden windfall. An invasion to a meaningful home or work place, or personal violation of safe space. A frantic call asking how fast you can get to the hospital.

Some sparks we control. Signing up for a first marathon. Buying (and wearing) a pair of red pants. Taking a day off. Getting a new hairstyle no one expected. Buying flowers, just because. Offering a random act of kindness or romantic invitation.

Some sparks we do not control. A global pandemic. A mid-season trade. The mercurial mood of our teenagers or world leaders. A stock market surge or dive. A hostile takeover. Degenerative eyesight, hormonal changes, osteoarthritis. A discovered duplicity, tragic accident, or terminal diagnosis.

The spark is merely the first, next phase of something continual and cyclical.

Consider the lifespan of any living organism. Trace the path of fledgling idea to billion-dollar industry, or how one voice alters an entire generation. Each example follows a similar story: something is born, interacts with its environment, takes shape, grows and matures, creates influence and impact, slows down, decays, and eventually dies. That which dies returns to its original form. A seed is planted for what may come next. A new space is opened, until it is ready to be filled.

The takeaway is that no spark, of any form, will last forever, however permanent we may first perceive it. With or without our permission, there's always another spark just ahead, brilliantly spurring our momentum in preparation for the next uncertainty.

Ironically for the super-driven, high-achiever crowd, the spark may arrive in the form of calm, quiet, open space. Many of us get so addicted to a 24/7, do-do-do pace, that a blank day on the calendar *is* a disruptive force. The day after selling the business. Passing a now-empty bedroom. The stark silence following divorce. The void after losing a loved one. Many of us get so performance-patterned in our sexual lives that we crave a spark of another form: heartfelt touch, co-created play, unleashed passion, surrender to a loving embrace.

The spark is neutral, neither good or bad. It has no inherent motivation.

We can generally find our way to appreciating the normal, necessary nature of change. Harder to comprehend is the *neutrality* of disruption. Do you ever find yourself:

- Thinking, "Surely, this _____
  (insert whatever spark has landed in your world) must have something to do with me, for me, or because of me, right?" Or, "What does this say about me?"

- Trying to influence and manipulate the world according to your own needs?

- Pausing to question your role, relevance, or (gulp) irrelevance in the vastness of it all?

At no point does the spark equate to, or infer, intent. This can be tough to grasp, as our default programming from birth associates disruptive change with pain. No newborn remains unfazed upon trading the comforts of the womb for the initially cold, clattering world. From that moment on, it's hard to not take change at least a little bit personally.

Yet some parts of us seek to ascribe personal meaning to these sparks, as if somebody, something, or the entire universe is acting according to our own inner dialogues:

- "$&%*(!#! Why is the world always out to get me?"

- "Whoop, whoop! I knew the world was looking out for me!"

Remember, the spark is just the spark—no more, no less. Winning the lottery is just as much a spark as losing your job. Whether we react by moving to negative, neutral, or positive squares is entirely our own doing (as we will find out further up the road).

*Allow the spark to fulfill its raison d'être:
the wake-up call to your next adventure, happening
right now, with or without your approval.*

• • •

REST STOP

Pause for a moment to check in with how you relate to disruptive sparks of change:

- What is your typical reaction to a disruptive spark of change? Do you approach with caution, gingerly tiptoeing around the edge? Are you practiced at pretending it's not there or fighting against it? Or do you welcome it with open arms and dive right in?

- Consider your current world of work, play, love, family, and friends. What disruptive sparks stand out from the last few weeks, or last couple hours? Note a few that come to mind.

- Is there one disruptive spark that may be inviting your next adventure? What might that involve? When might you begin? How might you start? (Hint: Yes, things are about to get messy!)

• • •

THE MESS

When prior balance is disturbed, order is set adrift. Any sense of normal becomes unhinged. As uncertainty rules, emotions get excited and exposed.

> Universally, the circle shape represents the present (and presence in the now), emotional connection, and completion of a perfect (or divine) whole. The single edge is smooth and soft, making it comforting to behold and easy to approach. The circle is not tied down and is designed for movement—rolling like a wheel; expanding and contracting, like ripples on water or waves of sound or data.
>
> The mess icon is composed of three circles that exist in disarray. The small, solid circle represents you and how you feel when that sense of prior alignment and harmony has been disturbed. Your position relative to the medium circle (representing those in your immediate span of influence) is in flux. Your position relative to the large circle (representing the higher order of things beyond your immediate influence) has shifted to the periphery. Yes, you are solid, but your relative place in it all is no longer centered.

After the spark, many signals mark your arrival in the mess. A first whisper of doubt or eager intrigue. The conversation that did not go as intended. A plan sliding sideways. Maybe the whole cart has been upended, fruit left scattered, bruised, and rolling down the road, for better or worse—only time will tell.

Whatever your state of arrival, that joy of effortless, enjoyable flow—at work, at home, in love, in play—has dissipated. That incredible period of harmony, or moment of pure awe, has come to an end. The spell has been broken, leaving you disoriented as to your place and the meaning of it all.

Welcome to the wonderful world of uncertainty and the emotional triggers that follow. Let's cover a basic orientation of how emotions work.

What we call "emotions" (anger, joy, calm, sadness, surprise, disgust, love, jealousy, and their many nuances) are merely best-guess adjectives used to convey the myriad of physical sensations we encounter in any given situation.

Ancient survival skills relied on speed over accuracy, so during periods of uncertainty or while under threat, we compute *meaning* from each physical sensation—within milliseconds. We then use that meaning to inform instinctual responses to minimize bad outcomes or maximize good ones. We apply that instinct when sensing similar situations the next time. And the next time. And every time that follows, if we perceive those instincts as advantageous.

But that legacy of instinctual emotional programming may or may not be *situationally* advantageous to our current reality. To share a personal example:

> As a very young child, I experienced the physical sensations that came with being hyper-aware and ultra-sensitive while witnessing unspoken tension between my parents. I might label those sensations as "worry."

> *When those tensions led to family upheaval and divorce (common early sparks and messes in many of our stories), with all the associated emotional turmoil, that feeling of worry became my instinctual response. I equated tension, in any form, to mean impending relationship breakdown that would lead to emotional neglect, rejection, and abandonment, a trifecta emotional state to be avoided, then and in the future, at all cost.*

I think you would agree that applying "worry" as the default association when encountering tension in *all* relationships going forward would be situationally disadvantageous. Instead, being able to engage in adult relationships while in the emotional mess of tension—at work, in marriage, as a father, with family and friends—has become an important and valuable ability leading to deeper emotional connection and breakthrough results. That does not mean "worry" was permanently erased from my psyche when things start to get messy. It just means I developed a fresher, stronger set of emotional associations—curiosity, alertness, compassion, conviction—to draw upon when navigating my way through anything that resembles relationship mess.

> *Emotions are powerful sign posts*
> *rising from your soul.*
> *They inform your way forward and*
> *light the way home.*

Just be sure to buckle up—the ride will not be smooth! As emotions start swirling, here's what to expect and how to keep yourself steadily moving forward.

Some part of you will feel "excited." That's a good thing.

Remember high school chemistry class when the experiment called for you to create an emulsion by "exciting" two liquids? Or imagine mixing olive oil and balsamic vinegar.

What we commonly describe as exciting (aka fun!) means our sense of normal has been somehow shaken or stirred. Remember that excite also means to agitate, provoke, and instigate. While being in the mess may well feel fun, get ready to have the less fun parts awakened too.

Maybe your experience will feel like a gentle spin cycle…or the vigorous shake of a snow globe, with all the bits and pieces swirling around a previously tranquil village scene. Maybe instead of a clear window, you're suddenly looking through a kaleidoscope, seeing refracted light—shards of colored glass creating brilliantly captivating, geometric patterns that draw you in, their meaning unknown. Or maybe you're staring into a bottomless void.

A tickle, trickle, or tsunami of emotion will follow. Don't fight it.

For some, the busier we get, the more we lose our inherent ability to *feel*. When truly absorbed in our own self-import, we avoid acknowledging our emotional states as if doing so merits a badge of honor. If a caring person or casual acquaintance asks, "How are you doing?" our standard reply has all the zeal of a wet noodle:

"Pretty good. Excited. Stressed. Things are interesting." Or just, "Meh." (Often followed by, "I guess.")

Other people wear their emotions on their sleeves. On a good day, our positive emotions radiate with all the color and brilliance of celebratory fireworks. On a bad day, our doom and gloom sucks the life from even the most optimistic rebuttal.

Whatever your inclination, the point is that your initial emotional reaction to being in the mess may leave you feeling raw and exposed. Expect it and roll with it.

And don't expect it to last.

Whether your version of messy is a welcome break from life before the spark or you find yourself clinging to a life raft, you won't be there forever. Our human predisposition is to return to a place of safety, security, and predictability. In that emotionally aroused state of uncertainty, whether or not we let it show, some parts of us feel exposed. Our critical-thinking, de-risking, problem-solving brains can stay on the sidelines only for so long.

At some point, expect that mental search for meaning to kick in. Imagine your brain receiving an all-points alert, summoning all faculties to:

- Identify the deepest place of emotional vulnerability.

- Find the quickest path to shore up that exposure.

- Start "fixing" a story that will return you to security, by any means necessary.

That's precisely what to expect as we move out of the mess and into the next step on the Adventure Arc.

※ ※ ※

REST STOP

TAKE A FEW NOTES AS A WAY OF GETTING YOUR EMOTIONS OUT AND visible, so you can see them and observe their true nature:

- What parts of your life are messy, in a state of flux, or being agitated or provoked?

- What emotions are rising up as a result? (Be sure to challenge your emotional vocabulary to use adjectives beyond "excited, stressed, and interested.")

- If your emotions were in liquid form, how would they taste on your palate? What color would they be? What shape would they take? If they had a voice, what would they say?

- Is there a current mess your emotions are asking you to pay attention to? Do you see a distant storm or tidal wave looming? Are you in the middle of one? Or have you matured through the lessons of the last one?

• • •

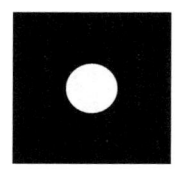

THE FIX

The mental grasp for meaning. The attempt to restore order and regain control. To protect what feels emotionally exposed, at all costs.

> In ancient times, the square shape was used to represent many important concepts: the past; the digestive system; concentration of will on a single point; force and protection by way of a solid structure, an immovable weight; and, because the square is designed not to move, decay.
>
> In our modern-day Adventure Arc, this symbolic meaning tells us everything we need to know. Technology taught us to hit the square button when we want playback to stop. The square in the fix icon represents a break, or halt in time, so we can digest what is happening. The inner circle represents you, fixed firmly within the box of your (possibly incorrect or outdated) learned thought processes and coping behaviors.

Get ready, fellow adventurer, this is the place where adventures can grind to a halt.

The mess puts the part of our brain responsible for critical thinking, de-risking, and problem-solving on high alert. Our human wiring is simply not programmed to withstand extended periods of uncertainty and emotional swirl. Motivated to escape prolonged messiness, our minds are prepared to leap over any inconvenient truths that interfere with the desire to preserve the "normal" we once knew—even in the face of irrefutable facts.

When confronted with the mess, we look first to the past for mental meaning and concentrate on a singular objective: to restore order in a way that we feel protected from unbounded emotional disarray. By filling in every square inch of open space with prior-learned experience, our logical brain feels solid and back in control…which tempts us to conclude what was true then also must be true for every experience to follow. (If only!)

The rush to replace all that uncertainty with what we *think* we know, or even more to the point, what we think we know *for sure*, paints us in a proverbial corner. With every square inch filled, we box ourselves in with historical thinking. It's a patch job at best, but in an effort to contain any further mess, we are incented to conclude that anything outside our box is either meaningless or extraneous, and therefore unworthy of further consideration.

*Overreliance on historical "meaning"
to make conclusive sense of messy emotions is
the common trap for all adventurers.*

So, as our brains work to restore order from disarray, we need to learn how to spot our mental attempts to force meaning so that we may disarm our brains quickly. Otherwise, we lock our growth in a box, impenetrable by fresh or contrary ideas. Here are the headlines of what to expect and the guidance you'll need to maintain forward momentum.

Our brains don't operate in isolation.

While navigating uncertainty, our superpowered mental-processing abilities work in relation to the sensory inputs received. That's millions of data points, across all mediums, everywhere we go, while awake or asleep, every hour of every day. This makes our "worlds," however you define them, vastly dynamic and complex. Too many permutations are continually happening to ever really claim to know *everything* there is to know about *anything*. But that doesn't stop us from trying.

Further, what we claim to *know* is never truly objective or complete. But while fending off any further emotional exposure that comes with *not* knowing, the critical-thinking brain doesn't want to believe that. It will happily *pretend* not to know even the most irrefutable of facts, and it will negotiate around any details that get in its way. When our brains are under duress, all those fast associations computed from past lived experience, no matter how biased or incomplete, will do just fine.

> *In the fix, we allow preconceptions to obscure facts, even the irrefutable ones sitting there in plain sight.*

Overreliance on past experience slows further adventuring, or even grinds it to a halt.

Being able to still our minds amidst a complex and competing swirl of messy emotions is the key to game-changing breakthroughs while on the adventure path. But until we experience mental stillness, and learn to trust it fully, expect what is commonly referred to as our logical, or "left brain," to clamor for attention. This is the brain's critical-thinking, linear mental functions pre-programmed to avert change, mitigate risk, and solve problems. That part of our muscle memory has an unquenchable thirst for certainty. It wants nothing more than to return all those stirred-up emotions to a predictable state, as quickly as possible.

Welcome to the inherent blind spot of our mental wiring: our ancestral bias for providing and protecting. Individual, familial, tribal, and species survival used to depend on the ability to systematically sort through data from past events to find patterns that helped us predict what was about to happen next. But by leaving no allowance for blind spots, or things we don't *yet* know, our first attempts to fix the mess actually weigh us down. Without realizing it, we become anchored in the past.

As perceived risk increases, the critical brain grasps for control by rapidly forming what it deems to be a conclusive understanding of the current situation. Yet this illusory "meaning," with all its learned oversights and miscalculations, is woefully incomplete. It leaves us playing small when facing bigger possibilities than we've yet to experience firsthand.

Of course, applying lived experience has some practical benefits—some lessons really don't need to be learned a second time. But over relying on past experience is akin to driving a car using only the rearview mirror; it sets us up for a very slow ride, on a collision course with a more serious reckoning that would otherwise be avoidable, if only we had turned our attention to the road ahead.

With our minds fixed in the gravitational pull back to certainty, get ready to face a formidable foe: FEAR.

The last issue relates to that hollow circle in the middle of the fix icon that represents you. Recall from the mess orientation that the circle shape also represents emotional connection, the present, and the completion of a perfect (or divine) whole. During the mess, whatever emotional connection is *most* present, *most* incomplete, *most* exposed for you is the one your mental capacity is subconsciously driven to *most* protect.

That part of the emotional core is responsible for concocting our most dire fear stories—the ones where all paths lead to the worst possible outcome and our ultimate demise. Social rejection and abandonment. The loss of autonomy. Insignificance or worthlessness. Being trapped in a humdrum existence, without the ability to express our most unique qualities.

When exposed, those parts of our emotional core—ingeniously equipped with all the hot buttons of our childhood bumps and bruises, trials, and traumas—trigger fearful behaviors that manifest in several common and recognizable forms:

- **F**rustration. Guarded and angry, of the repressed or expressed variety. Blaming others. Feeling like the whole world is conspiring against you.

- **E**nvy. Jealous, masking a yearning to belong. Coveting, on the outside looking in. All the while embroiled in anxiously protecting and perpetually pleasing others.

- **A**voidance. Juggling way too many balls. Diverted and distracted. Doing anything to resist or escape the reality of the present situation.

- **R**umination. Constantly critical. Recycling guilt. Resisting the reality in front of you by flipping between past regrets and future fictions (that always end badly).

And because our mental psyches are trained to build barricades to protect from emotional harm, those behaviors serve only to keep the better, fear*less* parts of our natures "boxed in."

> *Behind all fear lies one important truth:*
> *the next big prize awaits—right around the corner,*
> *and yours for the taking.*

Yes, being in the fix comes with a pretense of control and security—but don't be deceived. The harder you strive to shield your emotional core, the more you hinder growth and subject yourself to slow decay. Every seemingly insurmountable obstacle or big break*down* is actually your personalized invitation to a big break*through*. All you need to do is stay in the game and choose to adventure on.

If you take nothing else from this part of our basecamp orientation, take this: those fearful thoughts and impulses, acting as adventure detours and off-ramps, show up *precisely* when you've arrived at the doorstep of the next big move. You can be assured the path ahead leads to the heroic life you most want and were designed to realize.

* * *

REST STOP

FEAR-BASED ADVENTURE DETOURS AND OFF-RAMPS CAN BE TRICKY to spot, as they come in countless shapes and cunning disguises. However, each comes with a telltale sign: the internal whisper or shout of a fear story, which leads only to an endless dead-end loop or self-created quagmire.

Take a few minutes to reflect on which of these fear stories are most responsible for leaving you fixed in time, blocked from growth, and misdirected from your own adventure path:

- **Frustration at the perceived loss of autonomy.** Does fear ever whisper, "You'll never be daring enough," leading to an overzealous drive to be seen as impervious, in charge, and in control (of everything and everyone)? Do you equate vulnerability with weakness? Do others ever describe you as overcontrolling, guarded, or dominant?

- **Envy mixed with worry of social rejection and abandonment.** Does fear ever whisper, "You'll never be lovable enough," leading you to show everyone how nice, helpful, and giving you are? Do you equate service with self-sacrifice? Do others ever describe you as a pleaser, enabler, victim, or martyr?

- **Avoidance of the mundane, less glamorous parts of life.** Does fear ever whisper, "You'll never be special enough," leading you to chase one curiosity to the next, rebelling against anything that might slow you down? Do you procrastinate routine tasks? Do others ever describe you as distracted, hard to pin down, or full of nervous energy?

- **Rumination over past choices and future scenarios.** Does fear ever whisper, "You'll never know enough," leading you to strive to be right and relevant (in all things, to all people)? Do you circulate self-doubt? Do others ever describe you as overthinking, constantly critical, or a perfectionist?

Take a few moments to ask yourself:

- In what situations are your fear stories most present? In your work or career? With family and friends? As a parent, sibling, or best friend? With a spouse or lover? During the silent dark of your own 4:00 a.m. wake-ups?

- What roles, scenes, or entire scripts do your fears want you to rehearse or play out, again and again?

- As you let your mind play out a story, how does that story end? For you and for those around you?

- If left unaddressed, what sign posts of a more serious reckoning might lie ahead? Would your doctor, family, and closest friends agree?

• • •

THE CHOICE

The incarnation of agency. The option to either remain fixed by fear in a past that is no more or to trust our ability to move beyond fear and into the unknown.

> The triangle shape represents age-old meaning: the future, the nervous system, intellect, and truth. The triangle is sharp and conveys change and perseverance in risk. It is designed to be dynamic: stable when positioned on its base and unstable when positioned on any one tip. The triangle invites activation of agency and signals directional choice.
>
> The choice icon represents a necessary reorientation of the fix icon. The square shape of the fix icon is shifted ninety degrees in order to regenerate movement; it is split down the middle to form two triangles. One is filled in with everything you already know and points backward; the other is open to everything you don't yet know and points forward. This and that. Duality embodied.
>
> Notice the same open circle in the middle, symbolic of present emotion, whole, soft, and complete at the core, encapsulated in the forward-moving arrow—thus tipping the balance of open space slightly toward the future. Think of this as the invitation to engage

> your creative brain, to "push play" (another modern-day triangle reference), and to use your emotional core to chart a path onward, into the unknown.
>
> Which direction do you want to point your energy? The choice is yours!

Every adventure eventually leads to this fork-in-the-road moment of decision: follow the path of fear, fixed in the confines of that mental box (or block) of what feels safe and predictable…or let go and venture into the life you dare to dream.

This phase on the Adventure Arc marks another common thread in our collective human story, as depicted by theatrical plays, on-screen superheroes, archetypal characters in books, and mythical figures in songs and legends—across cultures, throughout time. Each plotline and each character's journey with fear brings up our most human of questions: am I enough?

In case it's not yet obvious, a resounding "YES!" is the answer. But for our purposes, we need to appreciate how fear will fan the flame of self-doubt every chance it gets. Deceptively disguised in cunning voices and forms, each whisper acts like an adventure off-ramp, or seductive shortcut, enticing your mind into self-absorbed, all-or-nothing scenarios that work only to subvert progress and distract you from the real adventure prize.

As you enter the choice, expect your favorite fear to show first as a fleeting mental blip. An early warning signal of an old wound about to be relived. As that perceived threat rises, the blip forms images, then video vignettes, and eventually entire plotlines. Left to its own devices, that fear story builds and builds until all you see is a bright red neon "DANGER" marquee flashing incessantly, manipulating your mental attention, monopolizing your energy.

Once hijacked, a fearful mind cleverly casts us into a scene, along with all the players around us, scripted by the classic roles of any good drama: the powerless victim, the treacherous villain, the idyllic rescuer. This fictitious mental theater distracts us from what's really going on. Left unchecked, fear redirects all our faculties to anywhere *but* the current reality. Even when things are miserable, fear can make crawling out of the warm, familiar bed of suffering too difficult. Pay heed, fellow adventurer, lest you stay stuck in a similar place.

Buried within all fear stories lies a singular motivation: to keep you from the prize of growing into the next special, daring, knowledgeable, and lovable version of who you were designed to be. In this moment. At this time. Fear serves only to disconnect you from the truth of your freedom, courage, and power, and the adventures you're meant to live.

> *In all its painful forms, fear is the antithesis of adventure —*
> *the downward spiral of isolation, despair,*
> *and perpetual suffering.*

I want you to know that this part of adventure is hard. It's about getting comfortable living *with* our fears and moving *beyond* them. At times that continual confronting of fear may feel like a battle with our innermost demons and, in some cases, like an epic fight to the death. And metaphorical death is exactly the outcome required for us to grow: the permanent retirement of an old fear association that limits what we believe about ourselves and whose past-due date has long since expired.

No doubt you've got your own lived experience with fear stories, detours, and dead-ends. Get ready to confront them again, but this time, you'll be better equipped to choose the lens through which to view them. You'll hold the pen to write a new plotline and story ending. Adventure invites you to mount your own private insurrection against fears of all kinds, relinquish their silent manipulation over you, and grow beyond them.

Otherwise, with fear at the helm, you'll try to sell yourself and anyone who will listen on why it's SO important for you to continually deviate from the adventure path. How you already have all the answers. How you're too busy with all the "should," "supposed-to," "have-to," and "need-to" urgencies. How it's your self-proclaimed destiny to do for others (what, in reality, only they can do for themselves) instead of tending to your own unfinished adventures.

Fears are the fictional stories we concoct when first confronting how little we actually know and control. Instead of halting momentum in hopes that fear will pass, an adventurer moves toward the prize and chooses to fear less.

Fellow adventurer, brace yourself for the real test.

The choice invites you to step into what exists beyond your frame of past experience and requires trust in your deeper intuition to point the way forward. Here are the headlines of what lies ahead.

Emotions are the prerequisite of movement, and they point the way forward (or back).

Consider that the word "emotion" is derived from the Latin "*emovere*," meaning to stir, to agitate, to move. So, what happens if we shut off, shut out, and otherwise subdue our emotional reactions? Movement of any kind is not possible, leaving us deaf, blind, and numb to the cues right in front of us (despite being obvious to others witnessing the same scene). If we deny emotions long enough, we languish in the mud while the rest of the world moves on.

Recall (from the mess orientation) that emotions are simply best-guess adjectives used to convey our physical reactions to any given situation. Emotions are also contagious, spreading and multiplying between beings. This holds true for the spectrum of positive emotions that point us forward and the negative ones that keep us stuck in the past.

This holds true for the strongest emotions (exhilaration, euphoria, ecstasy…rage, shame, despair), the more moderate (jovial, cheerful, sparkling…melancholy, grouchy, flustered), the subtle (serene, content, light…sheepish, cautious, wishful), and the numerous derivatives of them all.

Both positive and negative emotions serve as valuable signals, or cues, offering a glimpse into where one's current mental narrative is fixed. These emotional cues are easily translated by tuning in to the physical signs. However adept the mind has become at ignoring emotional undercurrents, the body can't be fooled. It takes notes, keeps score, and works methodically to balance the ledger. It sends the same loud signal, louder and louder, until someone finally pays attention.

Our physical beings have their own ingenious designs for keeping us tuned in to what emotions are most present, most real, and most worth choosing to move forward with. While we often miss our own cues, it's easy to spot them in others. Every good masseuse, physical therapist, athletic trainer, doctor, or holistic healer understands how emotions, if not expressed, become trapped in the physical body.

No physical cue is random. Those restless nights, 4 a.m. wake-ups, mood swings, aching back, headaches, bloated gut, tight muscles, waning or waxing sex drive, immobile joints, and nagging injuries…your body is calling, maybe even screaming, every way it knows how in order to activate a response to the deepest center of your emotional core.

Burying emotions while avoiding or negotiating with their physical representations is never a wise or sustainable strategy. Under sufficient pressure, emotions erupt in the worst possible ways, at the worst possible times, creating a reckoning causing all manner of pain and suffering for us and anyone in our paths.

> **GUIDE TIP:** Want to know how people around you are really doing? Don't fixate on the words they are using. Tune in to their tone and pitch. The energy they're giving off. Their body language. It's all there. Faint signals or flashing neon signs, vying for attention, trying to spur their own adventures, step forward. Or gauge your own emotional state simply by taking a long look in the mirror. Better still, strip down; observe how your body moves and reflects back at you. It will tell you the truth, clearly, courageously, compassionately. If you're ready to listen.

The key is to appreciate how emotions are meant to be "expressed." They should first be released, mined, or squeezed out, if necessary, and then observed, appreciated, and harvested for meaning. Imagine how a sommelier relates to wine. In a similar way, emotions are meant to be uncorked and set free to breathe. They are meant to be tasted and savored for their many properties and profiles—sweet, spicy, silky, or savory; light, delicate, elegant, playful, or juicy; dry, acidic, bitter, or tart; opulent, muscular, bold, or full-bodied; ridged, intense, or hot.

So, instead of thinking of your emotions as unimportant, "touchy feely," or something to be avoided, know that they are the all-important first step of putting your call to adventure into motion.

The choice of which emotional current to follow—positive emotions that open to the future or negative emotions stuck in the past—requires our creative-thinking brain to take the lead.

Recall that the critical-thinking brain, or so-called left brain, is what moves us from the mess to the fix by attempting to restore logical order following disruption. That is the part of our mental muscle memory we can't *survive* without; otherwise, we'd still be flailing around and adrift in the mess (which happens to some of us).

Problems arise by relying on one type of thinking over another. Honing only our critical-thinking functions leaves us going through life cut off from the entire other half of our mental abilities. The winning move is to build mental muscle memory in our critical *and* creative mental functions. Adventure teaches us to rebalance the equation.

The choice is all about dropping the old story of control, which means asking the critical-thinking brain to take a much deserved break. This is the time for its creative-thinking counterpart, commonly referred to as the "right brain," to take the main stage and lead the way with nonlinear mental functions preprogrammed with a limitless reservoir of imaginative, resourceful, and out-of-the-box tools. That's the part of our mental muscle memory we can't *grow* without.

We use the choice to reframe what the critical-thinking brain has determined "must be true" as simply an incomplete proxy based on our limited experiences gathered up to that point. That allows the creative-thinking brain to disintegrate our total picture of what is "right" into smaller pieces of what is "right now."

As our creative-thinking brains join the adventure, we begin to see things differently—and begin seeing different things. We open to what might *also* be "right," bringing lightness, fresh possibilities, and inspiring storylines. We start playing with which puzzle pieces to keep, which to toss aside, and which to create new purely through imagination. A new and exciting tapestry begins to emerge, a reintegrated total picture of what will come next. Woven into the fabric is the free, courageous, and powerful version of our beings that exist *beyond* fear. It's the certain path into uncertainty and the prize that awaits.

This phase of the Adventure Arc will be as short or as long as you choose to make it.

The accumulation of all that critical-brain processing and creative-brain exploring is necessary to move forward. How long we stand at the edge peering into the void is entirely our choice.

For some, being in the choice might involve years of painstaking buildup, fueled with anxious second-guessing or outright avoidance. Some fight to influence and manipulate the world according to their own needs, or they struggle with their relevance—or (gulp) irrelevance—in the vastness of it all. Yet, for those practiced in adventure, that same choice might entail a single night of soulful reflection before venturing into the dawn of a new day.

Big, heavy, nebulous stuff. Or light, playful, inviting stuff.

Depending on the adventure, we may find ourselves taking many small leaps, from one river rock to the next, or one giant acceleration, like a video game power-up mushroom. The choice is our own. Either way, the lens through which we choose to see the neutrality of the initial disruption that landed us in the choice allows us to immediately gauge:

Our comfort moving through fear into that which is not yet known (or unknowable),

AND

Our bias toward digging a deeper hole, doggedly clinging to what we *believe* to already know *for sure*.

This phase of adventure is all about trust. Not the misplaced kind, where we yearn to "trust" things will go on happening the way they always have. Or when we "trust" others to do what we want, when we want, and how we want, just so we can sidestep any real personal accountability or growth.

The choice invites (okay, requires) us to trust the age-old wisdom of our inner voice that knows a prize waits beyond anything the critical brain is capable of seeing on its own. As we find ourselves at the edge, peering down an unmarked trail or into a bottomless abyss, we trust in ourselves and in a higher order of things, unspoken and unseen. We trust that no matter what lies ahead, we'll be okay. That the resources and resolve required for us to stand tall and step forward will present themselves (as depicted in timeless quotes, metaphors, philosophies, and stories).

The choice requires us to surrender any last trace of perceived control; to view what might have seemed bedrock-solid as yet one more example of impermanence.

Expect to feel the weight of that reality sink in. Get curious about what might be possible *beyond* what feels known or predictable based on a still-evolving view of the world and the infinite complexity of how it works.

None of this is to suggest the choice should be forced. Recall from our initial basecamp welcome that rushing is the ruin of every adventure. Trust in patience and stillness. Don't make a move on the board, speak a word, or play a note that doesn't come from the soul.

Sure, invariably a time will come, perhaps sooner than we'd like to acknowledge, when there is no more evidence to gather, no more numbers to crunch, no more scenarios to evaluate. A point beyond which any reassessment is pure denial. At that natural boundary of "ENOUGH!" the choice is there to remind us that we have the intestinal fortitude, the backbone, and the balls to adventure on from what no longer serves our growth.

• • •

REST STOP

TAKE A MOMENT TO CONSIDER AND ANSWER THESE QUESTIONS:

- Where in your life might you be standing in the choice?
  In your career? With family? Physically? Financially? Romantically? Sexually?

- How long have you been there? Is your critical brain clinging to what it's always known? Or hard at work figuring out the sure path from here to there?

- From where you stand now, can you see across to the other side? How do things look over there? Do any fearful thoughts or full-blown stories keep coming up?

  Is the fear of feeling trapped, bored, or limited by realistic constraints tempting you to stay stuck in the box of showing your playful, spontaneous, and rebellious nature?

  Is the fear of feeling left out, rejected, or abandoned tempting you to stay stuck in the box of showing your nice, accommodating, and giving side to everyone around you?

  Is the fear of feeling unimportant, irrelevant, or worthless in the eyes of others tempting you to stay stuck in the box of proving how smart, right, and perfect you are?

  Is the fear of feeling weak, vulnerable, or overrun by external forces tempting you to stay stuck in the box of proving how dominant, large, and in-charge you are?

- If you drop the assumption, even for a few minutes, that more-of-the-same isn't the answer, what out-of-the-box alternatives is your creative brain capable of generating? Pick one that seems appealing—how might that storyline play out?

- If you were to make *that* choice, what prize (or prizes) might then be possible? What might happen in that moment of truth if you were to do any of the following?

Tear up the script or sign on the dotted line.

Pull the ripcord. Open up the throttle.

Deliver a vehement YES or declarative NO.

Try that thing you suck at. Publicly.

Ask for what you really want. This time in a single sentence, without all the explaining, justifying, or bargaining.

Admit your mistake. Let someone (maybe yourself) off the hook.

- Finally, if now is not the time to make the choice, then when exactly?

• • •

THE PRIZE

A return to balance. Celebrating the birth of a new and complete "whole." Centered in authentic and effortless connection with forces around you and beyond you. Life at its most brilliant.

> Recall what the circle shape symbolizes: the present (and presence in the now), emotional connection, and completion of a perfect (or divine) whole. It has a single edge, smooth and soft, unbounded and designed for movement—rolling, expanding, and contracting like a wheel, the ripples on water, sound, or data waves. It also represents the circulatory system—the effortless transmission, exchange, and spreading of all that is essential for life.
>
> Here at the prize, the same three circles of the mess icon are realigned, back in harmony. The small circle represents you relative to the medium circle (those in your immediate span of influence) and the large circle (the higher order of things orbiting beyond). You are emotionally centered and full, the embodiment of community. Your place in it all is restored, ready to radiate and receive the best life has to offer.

Imagine an invisible, heavy sack of stones strapped to your back. You're not a complainer, so you soldier forward, eyes on the prize, driven to accomplish serious and important work that impacts the lives of many. Over the years you designed all kinds of ways to compromise or shelve your own needs and weather the storm building inside.

But it's always there. From dawn to dusk and all through the night. After many years, you become convinced it's simply your burden to carry.

Then, suddenly, something changes. You can't quite put your finger on it, but everything just seems clearer, simpler, and easier. *Lighter.* People around you take notice. Immediately. They tell you so.

CHAPTER 2: THE ARC OF ADVENTURE   83

The heavy weight? Gone. You have been set free to enjoy the best in yourself in the full buffet of all life has to offer.

Congratulations, fellow adventurer. You've arrived at the prize! The *crazy good*, surreal stuff you've heard about but didn't imagine possible in your own life. The big payoff or ROI of your commitment to the adventure journey.

The prize is where you'll experience all you've been missing. The past becomes a ghost story. The future is left to unfold as it will.

This moment, the moment you
are in right now, is the only real certainty
you'll ever need.

Unlike those earlier adventure phases, the prize should be lingered in as long as humanly possible. Relish, savor, and devour every moment. This is where the finest parts of human design are united with the most precious gifts life has to offer. And before we get ahead of ourselves, here are the important realities to keep in mind.

The prize is about being with what is most real, not about chasing happiness.

Arriving at the prize awakens something innate inside us that has yet to see the light of day. Until now. Yes, you will shatter your prior definitions of fun, wonder, exuberance, and pleasure. And you'll also experience honest sadness, loss, and grief in ways you didn't think possible.

This is the thrill of inception, as truths from deep in your subconscious begin to take shape in the real world. This is when the stars align to deliver what you need. Almost by magic, the right person, epiphany, or resource appears without you asking or even thinking about it.

You'll experience what many describe as flow state, or what athletes call being in the zone. Everything slows down, your senses become acute with multidimensional clarity, and you operate on a higher plane. Like seeing all the moves on a chessboard in your mind before they happen. Or shooting a basketball from beyond the arc as easily as tossing a pebble in the ocean. Swimming with the current propelling you forward or riding a tailwind made just for you. Where playing, competing, or just being in the game of life is rich and rewarding, fluid and effortless.

At work, our ideas are clear and compelling. We make clean requests of those around us and team up to accomplish what wouldn't be possible on our own. Our execution is both disciplined and artful. We are accepting of where others are on their own journeys.

We are present with our families. Whatever the age and stage, humbled by the bond we share, amazed by their gifts, reveling in all they have to teach us. With awe, grace, and dignity we welcome new life into the world, provide guidance and support through important transitions, and walk others home to final rest.

Our best friendships and intimate relationships are rich. We listen beyond the words to hear the common story; we give voice to the deeper humanity. We radiate integrity, dependability, trust, and loyalty. We give freely and receive fully acts of kindness, wisdom, and protection. Our creative energy and sexual fire burn darkly and deliciously, with patience and passion.

Our energy is captivating, contagious, and restorative. We savor food and drink. We enjoy moving, challenging, and rewarding our physical bodies. We stimulate our minds as curious learners. We sleep deeply, our dreams lucid. We tune our spirits to forces in us, around us, and beyond us. Time ceases to matter.

This phase of adventure is where transformation is actualized, and yet most are reluctant to believe it is possible.

> **GUIDE TIP:** I've grown accustomed to skepticism when I share my own full immersion experiences in the prize—in team and solo competitions; in nature with other sentient beings; as witness to the joys and pains of endings and beginnings; exploring dark and light, yin and yang—all of it. The audience is captivated and inspired but somehow can't quite believe the same is possible for them. I smile, because that's what I used to think too. Believe it. Once you've committed to the adventure path, stay on the lookout for crazy shit to start happening. Don't want it to happen, don't wait for it to happen...just be ready when it does. And it always does.

Even in the prize you'll still notice the whisper of fear in the form of adventure off-ramps, seductive shortcuts, and distracting detours.

Remember, adventure teaches us to *live with* and *move beyond* our fears. We never fully shed them. Nor would we want to, as fears keep us sharp, keenly aware of the prizes we've realized and the paths that lead only backward. Perhaps you drive by an old drinking haunt. See a social media post from someone stuck in your old world. Suddenly you encounter an aggressive naysayer. Treat these as reminders of how far you've come, the life you might have had, the importance of staying committed to the adventure path, and the next challenge ahead.

Believe me, with practice you'll come to terms with old fear stories—greeting them with a knowing wink, brushing them off with a smile. You'll be able to acknowledge their origin stories. You'll appreciate the role they served in your transcendence into a person free from the weight of attachment and expectation. Courageous in how you interact with the world. Powerfully potent in your mind, body, heart, and spirit. So alive, you simply won't have time for all that old languishing, heavy wallowing, and circuitous self-doubt.

Nothing lasts forever, including the prize.

Soak it in, linger, but don't cling or get complacent. By now you have a deeper appreciation for the preciousness of life, your time on this planet, and the impermanence in all things. Just when things start to normalize around the next wave of safe, secure, and predictable, expect the disruptive spark to come calling. And when that happens (and it will), the cycle begins anew.

Fortunately, as you saddle up for your next adventure, you'll be that much more familiar with the entire Arc of Adventure, what to expect at each phase, and how to keep moving yourself forward, toward the next prize that awaits.

● ● ●

REST STOP

TAKE A FEW MOMENTS TO CONSIDER AND ANSWER THESE QUESTIONS:

- When in your life have you experienced the prize—moments when time slowed down or stood still and everything flowed seamlessly? In your work? With family, friends, or complete strangers? With a lover? In your experiences alone, wandering and exploring?

- What led you to those moments? Can you see how the entire Arc of Adventure led you there? An initial disruptive spark that wreaked havoc with life as you knew it? A critical-mind mental fix to restore some semblance of meaning? The choices that moved you into the unknown?

- What prize is visiting with you now? Are you embracing it for all it's worth, while it lasts?

* * *

WRAP-UP

With practice you will come to spot the Arc of Adventure and your current place in it across all aspects of your life. You'll also find it easy to see the impact of disruptive sparks on others and trace their progress through the messes, fixes, and choices of their own adventure arcs.

And no doubt, as disruptive sparks land differently on each of us causing adventure arcs to intermingle, you'll notice some folks—those most practiced at diligently progressing through each step of adventure—have a distinct advantage in the game of life. They are in the best position to guide themselves and others through particularly challenging times—a good reminder on the importance of staying in one's lane. Growth cannot be forced on those yet unable or unwilling to step through their own adventures.

Personally, I visit with the Arc of Adventure daily. A glimpse into my journal entries over the past week alone trace the impact of disruptive sparks that range from petty annoyance to pleasant surprise, from inconvenient reality to complete game changers:

- A bout of food poisoning
- Surprise outreach from an old friend
- A four-hour flight delay
- An unforeseen client opportunity

- A home break-in
- The news that the cancer in my father's bone marrow had evolved into leukemia
- The discovery of a treasure trove of lost childhood photos

Each event sparked a disruption to my sense of order, how the day was *supposed* to unfold, leaving things for better or worse in a state of emotional disarray. In each instance, my critical-thinking brain grasped to restore order and fix what felt messy, according to my terms of what was *supposed* to happen, how others were *supposed* to respond. And when things didn't go according to my master agenda, I landed squarely in that stuck place until I chose a deeper emotional current to fuel my way forward and ultimately arrive at the prizes awaiting:

A bout of food poisoning	→	A return to healthy eating habits
Surprise outreach from an old friend	→	Wise and timely counsel
A four-hour flight delay	→	A catch-up on creative writing
An unforeseen client opportunity	→	A bridge to next-level professional engagement
A home break-in	→	An aligned redefinition of home renovation

The news that the cancer in my father's bone marrow had evolved into leukemia	→	A soulful exchange and unwavering hug between father and son
The discovery of a treasure trove of lost childhood photos	→	The passing of stories to new generations

ONWARD!

In the third and final portion of basecamp orientation, you will learn all about the Axes of Adventure, the truth of your divine design, and how everything you need for a life of adventure is already prepacked, ready, and waiting inside you.

We'll have some fun journeying back in time to some of your early adventure memories, and we'll remind ourselves how our natural knack for adventure shapes our transition into adulthood. I'll highlight what's at risk when we stray from adventure and how adventure keeps us sharp and prepared for anything and everything that lies ahead.

CHAPTER 3

The Axes of Adventure

Our ancestors understood the world according to four essential elements: air, earth, water, and fire. Each held a unique set of powerful properties with rules that governed its nature. The potent vitality of water and earth were attributed to the divine feminine; the potent vitality of air and fire, to the divine masculine. These four elements formed the fabric of all things, of all beings. They were used to make sense of all manner of uncertainty and complexity, from solar systems and weather patterns to philosophy and artistry and the interactions between us human beings and our surroundings.

It was also understood to be problematic, even disastrous, for any one element to be overused in isolation or used to the detriment of another. To avoid any such polarization of extremes, each of the four elements was paired with another containing equal but opposing properties, which together formed a natural axis of harmonious counterbalance:

ALTITUDE

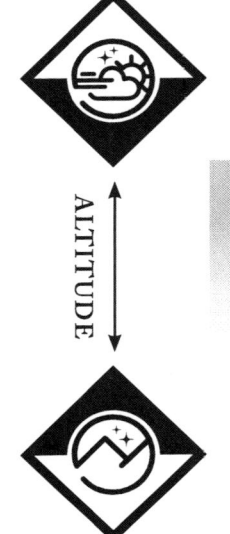

The opposing properties of AIR and EARTH are paired to form a counterbalanced "up-down" or "north-south" axis—your *adventure altitude*, used to maintain line of sight between future possibility (vision) and current reality (presence).

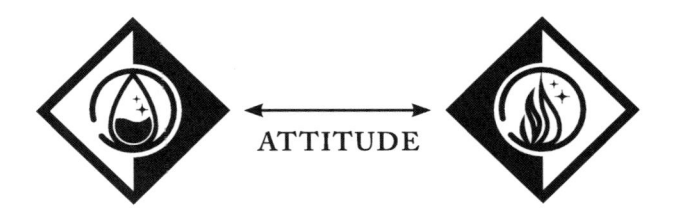

ATTITUDE

The opposing properties of WATER and FIRE are paired to form a counterbalanced "left-right" or "west-east" axis—your *adventure attitude*, used to amplify the impact of both loving kindness (empathy) and risk-taking (bravery).

Integrating each axis, with all four elements applied in equal measure, forms a complementary, complete, and indivisible whole that serves as a guidance system.

From ancient times to our world today, humans have used such systems to make sense of uncertainty and complexity:

- Explorers navigate the earth using longitudes and latitudes.

- Mathematicians and engineers map data in X-Y terms.

- Healers tap into a body's meridians.

- Business consultants assess problems and opportunities using 2x2 frameworks.

- Philosophers use terms like duality, Yin and Yang, and the "middle way."

- The rest of us communicate our relative positions using up-down and left-right, compass directions, or the hands on the face of a clock.

Whatever our orientation, we have learned to rely on such systems to assess our current positions in relation to where we most want to be. From there, we explore options, benefits, and risks, which inform how best to direct our attention and resources. Ultimately, we all face the same choice: go back, move forward, or do nothing.

For our adventure purposes, we translate each of these four essential elements and their respective axes into terms we can use in our day-to-day world:

Air represents **vision:** your innate ability to look up, dream, and imagine inspiring possibilities "outside-the-box" from any reality you've experienced so far.

Earth represents **presence:** your innate ability to stay grounded with reality, to focus on the facts, questions, and decisions most worthy of your best and complete attention.

Together when paired on a vertical axis, vision and presence represent your adventure **altitude,** which you use to maintain line of sight between future possibility and current reality:

Water represents **empathy:** your innate ability to feel the flow of kind and compassionate connections within yourself, with others, and the world around you.

Fire represents **bravery:** your innate ability to blaze new trails, take assertive action in the face of the unknown, and guard the boundaries integral to a life of noble purpose.

Together when paired on a horizontal axis, empathy and bravery represent your adventure **attitude**, which you use to amplify the impact of both loving kindness and risk taking.

CHAPTER 3: THE AXES OF ADVENTURE   95

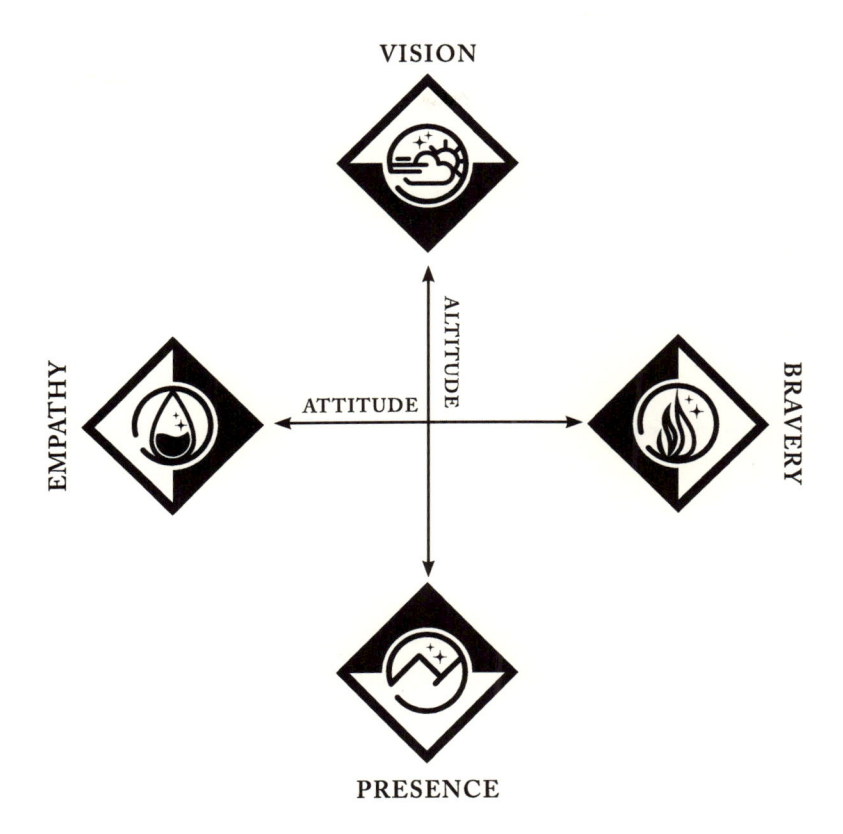

VISION

EMPATHY ← ATTITUDE | ALTITUDE → **BRAVERY**

PRESENCE

    I want you to think of vision, presence, empathy, and bravery as individual superpowers that live inside you—the four essential elements that come preloaded in your divine design, equipping you with everything you need for a lifetime of adventure.

    Each sits patiently in your corner, an ally wanting to be deployed into action, anytime, anywhere. In return, each asks to be nurtured and replenished, so as to be prepared to serve you to the best of its abilities in whatever adventure lies ahead. Navigating uncertainty, overcoming fear, and pursuing any form of breakthrough is possible only by harnessing the unique attributes of *each* of these superpowers *and* their codependent counterparts.

The pages ahead will cover a bit of important context for what we mean by "divine design." We will explore how we all adventure on autopilot during early and influential life experiences, shaping our relationships with the elements of vision, presence, empathy, and bravery. We'll then touch on how, during adulthood, we become susceptible to losing our way and how to get ourselves back on the adventure trail.

In the end, you'll come to appreciate how the ability to adventure, drawing upon each element of your design, is foundational to every aspect of the life you ultimately experience, in joy, in pain, and everything between. From your first breath to your last.

Let's roll.

* * *

THE TRUTH OF OUR DIVINE DESIGN: 101

The divine design of you, me, and every sentient being includes each of the four essential elements: air (our ability to have vision), earth (our ability to be present), water (our ability to feel empathy), fire (our ability to act bravely). These elements live inside you and, when activated, form a common bond among all things.

We could spend days on this topic alone. But as the final part of basecamp orientation, just a bit of context is all you'll need to get rolling.

First, don't let the word "divine" derail you.

We are referring to the innate characteristics that live within us all, that form our connections with each other, the world around us, and whatever exists beyond us.

You are free to attribute these qualities to whatever source you choose. Evolution. God or god. A creator. The cosmos. An inner soul. The Force. Or you can decide to just marvel and flow with it all and let the mystery be. We're not here to debate or judge.

By venturing into alternative definitions of the word "divine," we are invited to *delight*, *marvel*, and *find bliss*—all exquisite, pleasing, and awe-inspiring ways to think about the dynamic and powerful attributes of our human design.

> **GUIDE TIP:** Go further and imagine a divining rod, supernatural sword, or sturdy staff that guides your way forward as you deduce, perceive, and discover a deep and previously hidden power source—a natural, celestial current of elemental truth flowing within you that, once tapped, is never forced, never held back.

Second, for our purposes we're working with what is common in all of us.

A core adventure premise is that the divine feminine and divine masculine exists in all of us. Regardless of gender or sexual preference, by birth or by choice, we all have the capacity to summon the powers of vision, empathy, presence, and bravery as we adventure in life.

Our work here will not dive more deeply into themes of gender identity, fluidity, or sexual inclination. These important and intriguing topics are fully worthy of our time and attention but can be explored from other sources.

And finally, we're adventurers, not first-year medical students.

Hosts of other venues examine how the body responds to extended social isolation, prolonged periods of uncertainty, screen time obsession, negative news bombardment, nutrition, and activity (or lack thereof), the aging process, and so on.

What's important here is to understand that each of our four essential elements, these superpowers you're coming to know, are responsible for activating positive aspects of our brain chemistry and overall physiology. These free and naturally available mood-, energy-, and life-enhancing stimulants are available to you anytime, anywhere.

The more we adventure—by visioning inspiring ideas and possibilities; being present with our complete attention; forging empathetic connections of genuine kindness, love, and intimacy; and acting in brave and assertive ways—the more we release powerful hormones into our systems. Think of these as a supercharged mix that creates the perfect "adventure cocktail."

Dopamine starts the adventure wheels turning by fueling our drive to achieve and improving our attention span when concentrating on specific tasks. Testosterone enables healthy cardiovascular activity, improves memory and spatial reasoning, and boosts libido. A dash of endorphins works to reduce physical pain, raise natural immunity, and slow the aging process. No wonder we are so drawn to novel experiences, thrill seeking, testing our limits with nature, and bolstering our position relative to others.

The genuine, empathetic interactions between human beings—a knowing smile, heartfelt hug, or deep soul gaze—release oxytocin and serotonin (for giver *and* receiver), injecting that "feel good" aspect to our being. The same is true during interactions with animals and nature. It's easy to see why the desire for sunshine and pet ownership spikes during times of social isolation and works so well to reduce loneliness and depression.

Appreciating how this adventure cocktail continues to flow, when nurtured, even as our physicality declines through natural aging, is important. Think of all the legendary, inspiring people throughout time who have thrived despite crippling disease or traumatic accidents. Those who still innovate, challenge, teach, and heal. Commanding attention, respect, and admiration from all lucky enough to cross their paths. No matter the obstacles, they remain committed to utilizing all elements of their divine design, which keeps their adventure cocktails flowing, serving as inspiration to us all.

> **GUIDE TIP:** While all humans possess a similar makeup, the nuances of brain chemistry obviously differ from person to person. A deeper dive into your own physical and biological makeup holds only upside. Those who instead choose to stay ignorant about this stuff are literally shutting themselves off from decades of health and prosperity, while the best parts of life keep passing them by.

HOW ADVENTURE SHAPES OUR EARLIEST PERCEPTIONS OF THE WORLD, AND OUR PLACE IN IT

None of us get to pick the world we're born into. We get no vote when it comes to cultural background, socioeconomic status, birth order, genetic disposition…or even our names. We do our best with the hands we've been dealt. As we make our way in the world, many of us become aware of an inner voice that holds its own truth about who we *really* are.

This is the point in basecamp where "nature versus nurture" debates often get stirred up. To keep things straightforward, let's address all that hullabaloo in one fell swoop:

- You (me, and all of us) were born perfect, gifted with each of the four essential elements and the adaptive skills required to survive. Score one for nature.

- You (me, and all of us) were born into an imperfect world, full of joys and pains, traumas and tragedies, so adapt we did. Score one for nurture.

So, let's agree that from the beginning (or whenever you want to start the clock), the *perception* of who we are is built initially on both nature and nurture. Our parents, regardless of their degree of physical presence or emotional engagement, are at the center of influence. And yes, to all us fathers, the mother role holds more meaning in the early days. With each of our breaths that follow, innumerable "lessons" show up, derived from what each of our parents say (partially), how they behave (more so), and the size of the gap between their words and their actions (the most potent stuff).

Our parents first introduce us to the meaning, *their* meaning, of family, home, race, religion, and culture. The importance of work. The power of money. The role of relationships, laughter, love, intimacy, and sex. To all things healthy and harmful, and everything in between. Infinite interactions with these themes form our basic understanding of what life is all about and our places in it.

There's no other option, as we humans aren't much good at surviving without years of protected parental oversight. Luckily, we all are designed to learn, and learn quickly, by applying three basic incentives for human survival until we are old enough to fend for ourselves. We are driven to figure out:

- How best to seek and secure the good stuff: pleasure, attention, and love (and later on, sex).

- How best to avoid and guard against the bad stuff: physical, psychological, and emotional pain.

- How best to conserve energy through pattern recognition: formulating, storing, and relying upon early life hacks, so the same lessons need not be learned over and over.

With survival as the only master plan, we begin our grand adventures. As infants and toddlers, with each step we gather data and formulate conclusions—think "Energizer bunny" meets "insatiable sponge." We build layer upon layer of mental, emotional, and physical muscle memory. A sort of holistic scar tissue begins to form, calcifying all we are taught to believe.

Baby, you were born this way.

Childhood energy is custom-made for the adventure playground of our immediate surroundings, and we waste no time in testing our vision, presence, empathy, and bravery. Beliefs form with each and every lesson learned: the value of the pursuit of freedom and independence; how courage is used to build relationships; ways to gain and assert power. We trust those beliefs as we survive one adventure and move on to the next:

- Climbing out of a crib. Hiding in a closet. Holding a bug. Grabbing at an animal.

- Playing with our parts in the bath. Placing tongue on ice-cold metal. Holding hand over flame.

- Balancing on a teeter-totter. Tree climbing. Hill running. Stair surfing.

- Provoking a sibling. Emulating an adult. Apple polishing. Rebelling. Staging hunger strikes.

Teenage testing.

As teens, we adventure beyond immediate family and surroundings, probing the limits and boundaries of freedom, courage, and power. We seek to test ourselves beyond our immediate family constructs in ways that define our positions relative among peers and other adults:

- Discovering allegiances. Sorting out the cool and uncool.

- Getting picked—first, last, or not at all.

- Starting a fight. Watching a fight. Ending a fight.

- Seeing money. Stealing money. Earning money. Using money.

- Experiencing a first kiss. Seeing a sensual image. Having a sexual encounter. Feeling innocence, trust, shame.

- Being seen by a teacher or coach. Being celebrated, ignored, dismissed.

As we test ourselves, all the while we're refining our sense of meaning and relative importance of those essential elements of our nature:

- Our vision (expressing curiosity, imagination, creativity)
- Our presence (focused learning and achievement in the classroom, sports field, stage)
- Our empathy (tuned to social cues of belonging or betrayal, experimenting with releasing or burying emotions)
- Our bravery (testing rules, pushing limits, risk-taking)

Through it all, we're adding layer upon layer to our adventure playbooks. Without knowing it consciously, we learn how to confront the big concepts of life through these early adventures, forming the very fabric of our passages through childhood. At the heart of them all, we're testing and reinforcing our places in the world.

Roaring twenties.

Only by leaving the family nest do we begin to claim our own adventure storylines. Without fully realizing the significance, we strive to test our places in the bigger world, further stretching and building our adventure muscles around what it means to live the fullness of our freedom, courage, and power.

Is there any better time of life to savor adventure? Let the games begin!

- Summer jobs. College or not. Roommates. Sex, drugs, and rock 'n roll.

- Expanding the meaning of "home." Finding your own food. Creating your own style. Cleaning your own toilet.

- Making your own plans, with money, work, love, friends, nights, and weekends.

- Road trips. Concerts. Trains, backpacks, and hostels. One-way tickets.

- A taste of real romance. Opening, trusting, surrendering. A taste of real heartache.

- That first paycheck with your name on it. That first drive in a car you picked (and paid for). That first apartment with your name on the lease.

- Find job, then place to live? Find place to live, then job? Follow the money, heart, or head?

- More (better) sex.

- Monogamous? Move in? Marriage? Building the family you choose.

* * *

REST STOP

TAKE A FEW MINUTES TO GO BACK IN TIME AND RECALL YOUR EARLY adventure memories—the times, the places, the situations—when you had no master plan, no script, no playbook. The good times and bad, when you felt most alert and alive. Here are a few of mine.

Super Hero (age six). Alone and in charge, wandering to the abrupt end of subdivision sprawl. Drawn to enter the thick woods beyond. Finding just the right dead branch: a walking stick or spear to ward off a bear, or the sasquatch I saw on last night's TV episode of *The Million Dollar Man*. Later…a red towel tied cape-style, ready to burst into action. The television voice, speaking directly to me, "Chosen from among all others by the immortal elders, on a never-ending mission to right wrongs, develop understanding, and seek justice for all. Shazam!"

Unaccompanied Minor (age ten). Cross-country flights without an adult. Wandering behind row houses. Gathering discarded junk to build forts and hideaways. Poking a nest, fleeing the swarm. A plug of chewing tobacco. A pocket knife. The sight, smell, and taste of my own blood. Luring raccoons, mice, and skunks to wooden box traps, toppled by tugging a hidden rope. In the attic, a dusty stack of hidden *Playboy* magazines. Stealing candy. Bicycling everywhere and nowhere. Getting lost.

Budding Romeo (age fifteen). Long, longing gaze across the row of desks in homeroom. Butterflies. The cautious approach, through a best buddy. Notes of professed devotion. First dinner date. Dutch (whew). *Stairway to Heaven* or curfew? Kiss behind the gym. (Good choice).

You might want to categorize your adventure recollections by age: early childhood, teenage testing, roaring twenties. As you resurface the details of each adventure, jot down whatever comes up. Here are some questions to get you started:

- Which adventures most easily come to mind? Any you are personally proud of? Any do-overs you'd love to rewind the clock on? Looking back, if your adventure was a movie, book, or song, what would the title be?

- Do you see the arc your adventure followed? What was the initial disruptive spark? What felt out of place, uncertain, or messy? How did you attempt to fix things and restore order? At what point did you choose to see things differently? Did you end up experiencing a new version of yourself as a result?

- What elements of your design were engaged most: vision, presence, empathy, bravery? Looking back, which one or two did you rely on (perhaps more than the others)?

- During your more adventurous times, what adjectives or nicknames did others use to describe you? Do any of these validate or highlight certain parts of your nature?

And for bonus points:

- Choose people to share your adventure stories with: a sibling, longtime friend, your daughter or son, your partner, a parent.

Watch their reactions. See what happens when you invite them to get curious about their own early adventure stories.

> **GUIDE TIP:** If you're tempted to just keep reading without doing the work, remember why you're here. This is about reclaiming your sense of adventure, which starts by getting back in touch with what's inside you—your divine design. None of that happens without reengaging with the experiences and influences that shaped how you view yourself.

• • •

HOW WE LOSE OUR WAY

In modern Western culture, and increasingly around the world, other than organized religion (some of which are riddled with, even infested with, their own outdated doctrines and systemic abuses), there are few affirming rituals or "rites of passage" left to guide our transition into adulthood. Without this passing of the torch, the maturation of our divine design is often left to chance.

Precious few of us have access to a secure, mature, loving, local community of free, courageous, and powerful elders to support our transition. And the immediate bloodline of parental figures, despite the best of intentions, may not have the tools, time, or objectivity to steward our advancement into the adult world.

Without such guides, most of us are left to our own devices. Without the knowledge of how to make sense of our changing biology, from surging hormones to still-developing prefrontal cortex (the part of the brain that helps to inhibit impulse, feel remorse, and plan and align behaviors to achieve a goal), we're left to channel all that energy on our own.

> **GUIDE TIP:** Before we start the blame game, let's not heap all the fault on our mothers, fathers, and caregivers. They too were likely raised without the benefit of a community of present, inspiring, confident, wise, supportive, and loving elders. My own family story is full of men and women saddled with turmoil, grief, and unresolved suffering passed down the line from prior generations. From what I've garnered from their stories, I can easily imagine how the basics of securing work, food, and shelter for themselves and their families would overwhelm any formal rites of passage for the children they brought into the world. If we're going to blame them for all the bad stuff, we better be ready to credit them for all the good stuff too.

In a guidance vacuum filled with raging hormones, extreme media messaging, and the longing to fit in, we create our own rituals.

Even in less extreme conditions, left unguided, our adolescent uncertainty is inflamed by peer pressures and social media depictions. So, while perhaps not acceptable, it is at least understandable how young adults continue to act like children. Many of us are left to evolve without any protective boundaries or sense of morality, remorse, or repercussions.

We're all familiar with how this plays out. We engage in thrill-seeking adrenaline rushes, rebellious drinking, drugs, violence, sexual risk-taking and conquests, shame-inducing social media addiction, unhealthy affiliations—so often putting ourselves and others at risk.

These rituals become the de facto norms, the socially accepted rites of passage. Thankfully, most of us survive them. Tragically, we all know, or at least hear about, those who did not.

Without suitable guidance, we also are susceptible to suspended psychological maturation, which, while less physically perilous, gives rise to other forms of long-term risk and suffering:

- Confusion over the healthy expression of masculine and feminine traits, in the face of overly hyped versions of both in media and from influential figures in our lives

- Low self-worth that buries natural wants and desires under the weight of guilt

- The shame of inadequacy, early sexual exposures, generational frustrations, or even the mere presence of our most vulnerable of human traits

Amid the child-to-adult transition, complex themes emerge about how we are *supposed* to relate to our innate design. How we *should* think, feel, and act when it comes to family and community, work and money, the pursuit of loving attention and sex. At each step, for better or worse, we follow the path of least resistance by applying the earliest patterns we were taught as we carry out those same three basic incentives of human survival:

- Secure the good stuff.

- Avoid the bad stuff.

- Build patterns of recognition so we don't have to relearn the same lessons

When left to transition into adulthood on our own, it's not surprising we never fully leave behind the children in us. All those childhood lessons, cravings, desires, and fears sneak their way into the boardroom, backyard, and bedroom. When we come up against unfamiliar adult challenges, we revert to those same childhood strategies, rendering us woefully ill-equipped to deal with the issues of an adult world.

And you guessed it, when things don't go our way, the best of our divine design gives way to all sorts of unpleasant behavior:

- Petulance, pouting, and needy manipulation

- Impulsive escapism and insatiable cravings

- Overidentification with the importance of work, money, and sex

- Ceaseless striving, pleasing, and proving

- Misplaced anger, frustration, and blame

- Inability to give up control or keep our word (to ourselves, let alone others)

Now in adult-sized packages, with adult-sized effects, our fears run rampant in the world. They lead to grown-ups acting small, attempting to use and abuse their power over others, attracting other small-minded beings to their corrupted and toxic call.

As that internal tension rages, things spiral downward. We become attached to self-important stories. We live in scarcity and suspicion, drawn to using our power over others. We pour more of ourselves into bottomless voids and feel forbidden to breathe life into our most intuitive gifts, our most intimate expressions.

In our youth, we want it all. To be wild. Achieve significance. Feel love. Test boundaries.

*Those instincts don't change in adulthood,
but they do need to mature.*

As adults we intellectually know better, but inner conflict exists for as long as we carry unresolved pain. We try desperately to release that tension, reconcile the questions left unanswered, and heal the wounds of our youth. But without the appropriate tools and guidance, dissonant and harmful behaviors show up instead:

- **When someone or something doesn't act according to our master plans:** We get angry, frustrated, passive aggressive, or scheming, or we just plain attack. Anything to maintain the illusion of control.

- **When we hit a wall of reality we'd rather not deal with:** We create a distraction, procrastinate, rebel, or engage other forms of avoidance and escape.

- **When we feel gloomy, lonely, on the outside looking in:** We make ourselves feel better…down the whole bottle, eat the entire container, buy on impulse, binge-watch TV, or hide with porn to numb out. Anything to fill the void.

- **When we deny our natural gifts and successes and, yet, falsely believe we're somehow never quite good enough:** We work twice as hard. Make sure we get it right. Plan and perfect. Finally prove just how worthy we are.

Voila.
A world full of adults still behaving like juveniles.

Over time, the fear of losing what we think we own, control, or deserve, even after those things have grown stale or become harmful, overpowers the ability to dig ourselves out, shift gears, and rise to new opportunities. We get cunning and clever in our fight against change and retreat into youthful beliefs about our ability to influence an uncertain world. Too easily brushed off as "midlife crises," these slow-building reckonings are inevitable when we lose touch with the ability to adventure:

- **When our kids move on:** we cling to an outdated parental identity, discredit other interests and influences in their lives, and subconsciously subvert their independence.

- **When our partners take on interests of their own:** we resent their renewed passion and expanding connections while feeling badly about going for it ourselves.

- **When our parents initiate major change, become ill, or pass:** we deny or rebel against evolution in the family constellation.

- **When our worlds of work and wealth get disrupted:** we feel trapped in the careers and lifestyles we've perpetuated, imagining that more is the only way out.

- **When our bodies stop working the way we want them to:** we ignore the pain they carry.

- **When our sex drives aren't quite humming the way they once did:** we blame or hide in shame.

- **When our friends stop reaching out:** we self-isolate even further.

The longer we wallow in self-imposed confines, the more we lose the ability to reignite the best of our divine design and adventure mindset. At every predictable or unexpected life disruption that comes our way, we become agents of our own demise.

• • •

REST STOP

LET'S PAUSE TO REFLECT ON THE MANY INFLUENCES DURING THOSE formative years. Consider the people and development milestones that patterned your passage into young adulthood:

- Where did you do most of your learning? What was your "classroom?"

- Who were your "teachers?" How did their own choices, behaviors, and tendencies shape your way of seeing the world—intellectually, emotionally, physically, spiritually, sexually—for better or for worse?

- Were there one or two adults who served as positive guides during your transition into adulthood? Have you thanked them directly or by passing on what you learned to others?

Consider when, where, how (and for bonus points—why), in your maturation to adulthood, you displayed lingering patterns of childlike "acting out" in the form of immature behaviors or ineffective coping strategies:

- In your work or professional identity? In how you relate to money or wealth?

- In your family roles? With your parents and siblings, nieces and nephews, and your own children?

- In your romantic and sexual life? In the pursuit, enjoyment, or avoidance of intimate emotional and physical connections through marriage or partnership?

What parts of your life today feel more or less tuned in to an adventure mindset? When you look closely, can you spot any signs of a slow-building crisis? Or are you staring down a full-blown reckoning?

• • •

HOW TO GET IT BACK: FROM THE FIX TO THE CHOICE

It is important to realize that from time to time we *all* lose our way. Fear, in one form or another (frustration, envy, avoidance, and rumination), has a way of catching us all off guard, luring us backward or sideways, down endless detours away from the adventure path.

The cause is simple: fear triggers an overreliance on any one of those essential elements (vision, presence, empathy, bravery), first to the detriment of its complementary counterpart and ultimately to the rest of our divine design.

Recall that on the Arc of Adventure, following any disruptive spark, we enter that messy period where things are in disarray. Our mind, triggered by fear of one kind or another, seeks a quick fix to return some semblance of control and order, using the richest vein of source material available: our childhood patterns.

Recall also that all four of our superpowers were designed to coexist, creating the axes of adventure.

When facing fear-rousing uncertainty, consider how we might grasp for meaning by over relying on one or two elements that have become patterned as the default fix in similar situations up to that point. Sure, it may feel like order is restored, but in fact we have boxed ourselves into the same corner by failing to draw upon all aspects of our divine design. Here's how that might play out.

Our adventure attitude is diminished when we either:

- Over rely on bravery (to the detriment of empathy), like belligerent bullies clinging to control, blind to the impact of our anger on others or ourselves (**F**rustration); or

- Over rely on empathy (to the detriment of bravery), like perpetual pleasers endlessly serving others while our own dreams and desires drift away (**E**nvy).

Our adventure altitude is compromised when we either:

- Over rely on vision (to the detriment of presence), like distracted jugglers swept away with grand schemes or new possibilities to escape painful realities or the perceived boredom of staying on task (**A**voidance); or

- Over rely on presence (to the detriment of vision), like constant critics stuck in the weeds overanalyzing while losing sight of the big picture (**R**umination).

The good news is that regardless of the depth of transgression, we all have the ability to shift our perspectives and rebalance our adventure altitudes or attitudes, as the case may be. The choice is our anytime/anywhere invitation to make situational course corrections by reengaging the underutilized aspects of our nature.

Here is your roadmap primer when arriving at any decision point along the adventure path.

Raise your adventure altitude: when to choose vision.

The air/vision element addresses the basic human need to feel limitless and extraordinary. It taps into our spirit energy and the natural capacity to express creative curiosity, playful improvisation, and innovative resourcefulness.

As a common first move when embarking on any adventure, we use vision to look skyward and dream up possibilities for a better future, beyond any reality experienced so far.

On the adventure path, use vision to ask and answer the question: "What inspiring idea is calling to me?" When you're stuck, vision frees your mind to think outside the box, see around corners, and see through obstacles. When times get tough, it's how we maintain faith and keep our resources trained on the big prize.

Focus your adventure altitude: when to choose presence.

The earth/presence element addresses the basic human need to know we are standing on solid ground. It taps into our intellectual energy and the natural application of mindfulness, objective investigation, and disciplined execution of the priorities required to accomplish our visions.

A common choice when overwhelmed with ideas or options, presence keeps us grounded on facts and attending to detail. We use it to explore deeper truths, restore calm, and channel wisdom.

On the adventure path, use presence to ask and answer the question: "What topic, question, or decision deserves my complete attention at this time?" When you're stuck, presence helps you get clear and directs your intellectual faculties toward achieving what matters most.

Soften your adventure attitude: when to choose empathy.

The water/empathy element addresses the basic human need to belong, to be seen and cherished as whole, perfectly imperfect, and complete as we are. It taps into heart energy and the natural desire to feel genuine, compassionate connections within yourself and between those around you.

A common choice when numb, walled-up, or blocked, empathy keeps us honest with the emotional currents flowing in us and around us. We use it to engage in deep listening and to intuit when, where, why, and how to offer and request acts of kindness, love, and intimacy.

On the adventure path, use empathy to ask and answer the question: "What emotional current is most active in me and around me?" When you're stuck, empathy helps you to slow down, wash away frustration and heaviness, and trust your heart with laughter and lightness.

Strengthen your adventure attitude: when to choose bravery.

The fire/bravery element addresses the basic human need to live life fully, independently, and autonomously, on our own terms. It taps into our body energy and prepares us to blaze new trails that manifest our own dreams, feelings, and priorities in the physical world.

A common choice when approaching something new or making a bold leap into the unknown, bravery burns through the clutter of the past and keeps us active in pursuit of what lies ahead. We use it to release all that no longer serves our growth, to show strength through vulnerability, and to champion a life truly worth living.

On the adventure path, use bravery to ask and answer the question: "To live on my terms, what am I willing to let go of and step into?" When you're stuck, bravery helps you challenge limits, harness grit and resolve, discern boundaries, and pay the price required to pursue the life you most want.

> **GUIDE TIP:** Notice that each essential element icon borrows from the choice icon: the fixed, blocked, immovable square shifted and reimagined as two triangles. One triangle, filled in with everything you already know, points backward; the other triangle, open to everything you don't yet know, points forward. On the adventure path, each element is available to engage with in one of two ways. By pointing that energy backward, you'll stay stuck in the fix, wandering endless detours and dead-ends. By pointing that energy forward, you'll be back on the adventure path, one step closer to new joys awaiting.

* * *

REST STOP

As we bring our basecamp orientation to a natural close, now is the perfect time to take stock of the many aspects of your life currently in play. Some you may be pursuing in parallel while others may feel in conflict. Begin by considering the big energy expenditures—external impact; meaningful relationships; personal fuel—and the sub-categories within each. Feel free to add your own:

- External impact (professional, career, or community)

  Intellectual challenge and stimulation

  Creative expression and enjoyment

  Trusted bonds with colleagues and contacts

  Financial prosperity, recognition, and reward

  Soul alignment to personal mantra, mission, and sense of purpose

  Access to future paths and growth

- Meaningful relationships (family and friends of origin or choice)

  Spouse/partner (trust, communication, emotional and sexual intimacy)

Mother (nature of memories and/or current connection)

Father (nature of memories and/or current connection)

Children/minors (appropriate level of parenting and/or caregiving)

Siblings and extended family (role in your life then and/or now)

Longtime, close, trusted friends (role in your life then and/or now)

- Personal fuel (the stuff that keeps your tank full)

    Physical fitness and body health

    Mental health and emotional well-being

    Ease of giving and receiving acts of support, kindness, and intimacy

    Spiritual connection with forces beyond yourself

    Hobbies and pursuits of pure fun, play, leisure, and joy

    Sense of worth and self-regard

As you take an honest stroll through the sub-categories, ask yourself: Which ones jump off the page as most worth celebrating? Which ones fall flat? What do your eyes prefer to skip over?

Recall that the true Anatomy of Adventure stems from paying attention to see disruptions as personally fortuitous moments in time designed to invite your growth. Is there *one* most in need of a wake-up call?

Next build some practice in understanding your place in the Arc of Adventure. Apply the appropriate Arc icon or use another notation scheme that works for you (a check mark, "X", "!!!", or "?"; different highlighter colors) as you ask yourself, in this moment:

- Which *one* has you experiencing the prize of feeling most fully alive?
- Which *one* is being visited by the most disruptive spark?
- Which *one* feels the messiest?
- Which *one* has you most fixed in the past, stuck, or completely boxed in?
- Which *one* is most inviting your choice to embark on a new adventure?

For bonus points ignite your adventure engines by also asking: "Which leaves me feeling…" after each of your answers above. Remember the equation: no emotion equals no forward progress.

Now pull from what you know about the Axes of Adventure and the essential elements of each. In your journal or in the margin take notes as to the specific evidence you see of:

Living with your adventure altitude (vision and presence) in balance OR over relying on one element (which one?). Where might it be time and/or what might happen if you were to:

- **Choose to elevate your adventure altitude by engaging more vision.** Get your head out of the details, lift your spirit skyward, and imagine unbounded possibilities ahead.

- **Choose to focus your adventure altitude by engaging more presence.** Come back down to earth, get clear about the reality of the moment, channel your resources to only that which is most deserving of your complete attention.

Living with your adventure attitude (empathy and bravery) in balance OR over relying on one element (which one?). Where might it be time and/or what might happen if you were to:

- **Choose to soften your adventure attitude by engaging more empathy.** Tune into the emotions inside you, the ones flowing strongly, the ones blocked from being expressed.

- **Choose to sharpen your adventure attitude by engaging more bravery.** Trust the fire of your own flame, burn through the rubbish, step into conflict, assert the boundaries that honor your autonomy.

* * *

PART 2

THE THREE GREATEST ADVENTURES

As you prepare to embark on the three greatest adventures, let's make sure you have everything you need.

QUICK REFERENCE GUIDE

1. **The Freedom Adventure is the path to authentic independence.** On this adventure you will learn to:

    Derive new meaning from your past. Master your strengths and fears to be clear in all you do and in the wake you leave behind. Trust your own mantra in life, breath to bone.

2. **The Courage Adventure is the path to collective prosperity.** On this adventure you will learn to:

   See and savor the essence of life around you. Accept and acknowledge differences, above any need to control. Choose how best to engage and thrive in a world of relationships.

3. **The Power Adventure is the path to vital renewal.** On this adventure you will learn to:

   Prime your potency. Stoke your wildfire. Rejuvenate the essential elements of your nature, beyond the security and limits of who you were. Embody and celebrate the sanctity of life.

THE ORDER MATTERS (START WITH FREEDOM)

Regardless of age, stage of life, and current situation, you'll never go wrong by starting with the Freedom Adventure. Establishing or reestablishing a fresh perspective of who you are *now*, what independence is all about at *this* point of your life, and trusting your *present-day* place in the world, is foundational to everything that follows.

Recall that each of the three adventures are designed to prepare you for what comes next. Going in reverse order or skipping one of the adventures won't work:

- Claiming your authentic independence on the Freedom Adventure is prerequisite to the pursuit of collective prosperity on the Courage Adventure. Said another way, you'll need to *know* who you are before you can *show* who you are to the world.

- On the Courage Adventure, your newfound freedom will be put to the test as you enter the world of relationships and begin to collaborate, create, and achieve beyond anything you're capable of alone. And after a time, as stagnation starts to creep in, you'll feel the pull to *grow* who you most want to become by leveling-up in the Power Adventure.

- Once rejuvenated, power tanks full, you'll be ready for a rebirth—a fresh and evolved definition of who you are *now*—by taking on the Freedom Adventure, once again.

The three greatest adventures work as a continual circuit—freedom leads to courage, courage leads to power, power leads to renewed freedom—to traverse, complete, and begin anew, many times over a lifetime.

YOUR TRAIL GUIDE TO ADVENTURE SUCCESS

Remember, adventure entails letting go of what you already know. That means the way forward will be bumpy, baffling, and not always clear. Expect fear to clamor for your attention and divert your best intention. The key to steady progress is treating each step forward as an investment, not as an expense or opportunity cost. It means trusting in yourself, creating and spreading prosperity, and staying relevant in the world around you.

Each adventure is laid out in a consistent flow so you can establish a familiar pattern as you progress. In each chapter ahead, you will find:

- Highlights of the big prizes and payoffs waiting for you on the other side

- Risks entailed with not completing the adventure

- An overview of what the adventure is all about

- A preview of what will be hard at first, until it's not

- A simple warm-up before setting off

CREATE YOUR OWN ADVENTURE

You'll then be presented with a series of short expeditions that make up the broader adventure. Think of these as progressive stages preparing you for what comes next. (Again, you guessed it, the order matters.)

I'll keep posting guide tips along the way, along with a few activities to engage with at whatever dose, manner, and pace feels right. This is your opportunity to do as much or as little as you choose. Don't expect to be spoon-fed, and be mindful to not start overthinking, overimagining, or overcontrolling before you get off the starting blocks. Just get yourself moving, and the rest will unfold from there.

A QUICK NOTE ON PRONOUNS

My intention in basecamp is to welcome new arrivals into a gathering place that feels individually energizing and collectively hospitable. Gathering any collection of people together comes with some level of inherent diversity, so I tend to use "us, we, and our" as the means to invite each adventurer to find personal connection within the communal orientation. I may stray here and there, but that's the idea.

Moving into the greatest three adventures, I blend "us, we, and our" with "you and your" when describing the payoffs waiting on the other side. This is to reinforce inclusiveness and open more personal connection with the common human story. I invite all readers to find their own positive and rightful places in a way that celebrates similarities *and* differences. That kind of energy is contagious, motivating, and valuable on any kind of adventure.

You may notice my pronoun choice shifts when outlining the risks entailed with not completing the adventure—as that part is all about you. After all, *we* can plan, prepare, and problem-solve, but only *you* can own how to think, feel, and act. Only *you* can own the decision on timing, direction, dosage, and readiness. Understand that this shift is intentionally provocative and may leave you feeling suddenly alone in the hot seat.

Also, know this shift is **not** done to trigger guilt over all the things you haven't realized (yet) or to suggest that some part of you is seriously broken beyond repair. Quite the opposite. Adventures are all about stripping down the distractions and getting to the heart of the matter to liberate your freedom, courage, and power…to *your* advantage. That means using this book as a proxy for holding up the mirror to reveal that most meaningful and soul-empowering conversation you must have with yourself.

You will notice I continue that approach in the preview of what will be hard (at first), the warm-up, and all of the adventure stages that follow. Again, I may not get it perfectly, but I invite you to trust and work with my intentions.

Keep your focus on the big picture we've established. Yes, adventure is an "inside job." When the going gets tough, no one can do the work for you, making the adventure trail feel solitary at times. Remember, you're only as lonely as you decide to be. In reality, you are forever surrounded by other adventurous souls going through their versions of the same stuff— a comforting thought to keep close during good times and bad.

PACK LIGHT

Pick up a new journal, adventure logbook, or whatever else works to track your progress. Believe me, you'll appreciate having a record to look back on in the months and years ahead.

Dump any extraneous baggage and weight (literal or metaphorical). Trust yourself with everything you learned in basecamp orientation. You can refer back to any specific section or the big takeaways anytime you need to:

- Embrace your new definition of the Anatomy of Adventure

    I choose to see each new disruption as a personally fortuitous moment, an invitation to grow beyond and into unknown thrills ahead.

- Follow the Arc of Adventure

    The Spark: The ground zero of every adventure. When disruptive change comes calling, small or significant, by random chance or intentional design.

    The Mess: When prior balance is disturbed, order is set adrift. Any sense of normal becomes unhinged. As uncertainty rules, emotions get excited and exposed.

    The Fix: The mental grasp for meaning. The attempt to restore order and regain control. To protect what feels emotionally exposed, at all costs.

    The Choice: The incarnation of agency. The option to either remain fixed by fear in a past that is no more or to trust our ability to move beyond fear and into the unknown.

The Prize: A return to balance; the birth of a new and complete "whole." Centered in authentic and effortless connection with forces around you and beyond you. Life at its most brilliant.

- Navigate the road of uncertainty using the Axes of Adventure, and choose to move forward through fear by using the essential elements already inside of you

    Use vision to ask and answer the question: "What inspiring idea is calling to me?" When stuck, vision frees your mind to think outside the box, see around corners, and see through obstacles. When times get tough, it's how you keep the faith, with your thoughts, feelings, and actions all targeted on the big prize.

    Use presence to ask and answer the question: "What topic, question, or decision deserves my complete attention at this time?" When stuck, presence helps you get clear and direct your intellectual faculties toward achieving what matters most at any given time.

    Use empathy to ask and answer the question: "What emotional current is most active in me and around me?" When stuck, empathy helps you slow down, wash away frustration and heaviness, and follow your heart with laughter and lightness.

    Use bravery to ask and answer the question: "To live on my terms, what am I willing to let go of and step into?" When stuck, bravery helps you challenge limits, harness grit and resolve, discern boundaries, and pay the price required to pursue the life you most want.

CELEBRATE WITH YOUR OWN
GIFT OF COMPLETION

Finally, each of the three greatest adventures concludes with a rite of passage. Have fun with these. Make them your own. Share them with others. This is your opportunity to commemorate how far you've come in a way that is lasting and meaningful to you.

• • •

You've done your best living in an outdated version of who you really are.

It's time to know yourself more fully and trust your independent place in the world.

But your definition of freedom is incomplete.

Until now.

CHAPTER 4

Welcome to the Freedom Adventure!

Imagine a version of your life where you don't second-guess yourself. EVER. A deep sense of belonging: in each moment, with each moment, for each moment. Tuned in. Complete, capable, and clear. Calm and strong:

- At work.

- With money moves.

- When making any decision.

- In your most intimate relationships.

- With family and friends.

- When carving out time just for yourself. (And if you don't regularly do this, you will soon!)

The joys of claiming, or reclaiming, your true independence are immediate and immeasurable. Here are some of the payoffs you can look forward to.

AS INDEPENDENT BEINGS, WE TRUST OURSELVES AND OUR PLACES IN THE WORLD

That is how we are able to enjoy our life accomplishments, pursuits, shortcomings, and slips without being swept away by the highs or devoured by the lows. We don't take ourselves so seriously that everything feels personal. We don't get caught up continually defending, explaining, or justifying.

Those truly free live with a high degree of self-awareness. We are able to self-regulate desires, impulses, and fears, so as to act in authentic congruence with our surroundings, whether or not anyone is watching. We hold our uniqueness with respect, dignity, and honor and don't feel confused or conflicted about:

- **Our family of origin.** We choose the gifts and attributes to bring forward. We release former transgressions, so as not to carry on old wounds or pass them further down the line.

- **Our family of choice.** We cherish our ability to attract and revel in the close camaraderie of others. We share laughter, wisdom, support, and intimate connection, beyond the bond of blood.

- **Our personal vision of a life worth striving for.** We know where, how, when, and why we "belong." We trust our charismatic agency to create and seize opportunities. We prioritize self-care, asking for (and accepting) help when in need. We value our alone time and solo pursuits.

- **Our feminine and masculine power.** We honor and harness the full spectrum of their respective qualities by balancing compassion, vulnerability, and flow with assertiveness, accountability, and boundary. We own our creativity, decisions, and sexual fire (so it doesn't own us), never hiding or coercing, bargaining or manipulating, or just "going along."

- **Our desires in life.** We hold unwavering devotion to following our passions and refining our skills. We channel our resources to earn, enjoy, and share financial prosperity, spreading our currency into the expansive ecosystem of human exchange.

OUR AUTHENTICITY MAGNETICALLY ATTRACTS OTHERS

Even those independent beings we may not agree with or choose to follow command our attention and induce our respect and admiration. Not surprisingly, comfort with one's strengths in the world, uncompromising integrity, and relentless commitment to soulful expression are alluring qualities—professionally, personally, and romantically.

As a friend of mine who knows a thing or two about the fluid and primal attraction between genders is fond of saying, "There's nothing sexier than authenticity."

A FREE PERSON DEMONSTRATES TRUE LEADERSHIP BY FIRST LEADING THEMSELVES

Authentic people tend to the important work of getting clear with themselves before aspiring or attempting to lead others. They treat their commitments to themselves like gold. When others witness that kind of personal integrity, it's all the evidence they need to trust their word and follow their lead, directly or indirectly.

The opposite is equally true. Inauthentic, disingenuous people may be initially seductive in their rebellious nature or too-good-to-be-true promises of a better future. But those who propagate a brand of living that they themselves don't follow are destined to squander their leadership stances (likely sooner than later).

FREEDOM BEGETS FREEDOM

Like attracts like. Patiently and diligently tending to our own freedom garners the respect of others. During and after the Freedom Adventure, we find ourselves increasingly surrounded by those with their *own* brand of authentic independence. Imagine how amazingly rich and rewarding life gets when we're encircled with the company of such people (and distanced from those who drain our energy with their own needy attachments, expectations, and dependencies).

The fact that authenticity is contagious creates the biggest short- and long-term payoff to the Freedom Adventure. All people we affect, directly or by extension, have their own subconscious agendas: they want what we have! That is, they want to find, claim, and experience their *own* unique brand of freedom.

And the best part is that we don't have to *do* anything to help them achieve it. We just need to heed the call of our own Freedom Adventure and claim our authentic independence, trusting ourselves in each moment, for each moment.

That's more than enough to model the way for others.

THE RISKS OF NOT COMPLETING
THE FREEDOM ADVENTURE

Without realizing your authentic independence...

*the inner workings of your childhood wiring
will stifle your adult world.*

*You'll be like a puppet on strings, at the mercy
of your subconscious puppet master,*

*with a life mired in self-doubt, all tangled up
in the web of someone else's script.*

WHAT DOES IT LOOK LIKE WHEN YOU ARE NOT LIVING WITH REAL FREEDOM?

In a word: **attached**.

Without freedom, you're forever seeking to find, define, and value yourself through the eyes of others. Each and every time, you'll come up short. Flummoxed, anxious, and insecure. Without realizing it, you will be the author of your own demise.

Without claiming your freedom, you'll subconsciously manage the day-to-day, approach key decisions, and choose life paths based on the expectations, values, and beliefs passed down to you from others—right or wrong, for better or for worse, knowingly or unknowingly.

If you are anything like me (and every person I know), somewhere in your late teens or early twenties, you headed off into the world, bound and determined to follow your own independent path. We all do so largely blind to our underlying childhood stories still very much in play. Left unchecked, these stories shape your young-adult experiences and decisions, big and small.

In simplest terms, each of us leaves the nest either:

Believing (even idolizing) the legacy family values and parental influences. In which case you use *matching* reference points to filter, make sense of, and create your early adult encounters with big life themes related to education, work, money, relationships, status, and sex;

> OR

Rejecting (even demonizing) those same values and influences. In which case you use *opposing* reference points to filter, make sense of, and create your early adult encounters with big life themes related to education, work, money, relationships, and sex.

Either way, you embark on adulthood
under the illusion of independence,
while in truth still governed by the world
you thought you'd left behind.

Dogged determination to live out either playbook means you will never find security with yourself. A lifetime of detours and dead-ends await if that inner tension is not addressed and resolved. The path to authentic freedom requires you to shake family idols off the pedestal and/or release family demons from the gutter.

Think of the Freedom Adventure as your big moment to write, or rewrite, your *own* story. All you really need is a quiet place, a blank page, and a humble pen. But failing to do so comes at great cost. Here are some of the risks you face by not claiming your freedom.

Without the Freedom Adventure, you are destined to replay the story of your father, mother, or prior generations—this time recast with *you* in the starring role.

Reading from someone else's script, adopting the trials and tribulations of a life not your own, is a weighty, sad, and ultimately losing proposition. It's a path of ceaseless striving, perpetual pleasing, and outward frustration borne of internal tension.

No matter what you do, driven with that form of externally defined self, you'll never be quite _____ enough (fill in your own blank). It's a one-way ticket to imposter syndrome, like being trapped in a shell or shadow, leading to an exasperated life left unfulfilled.

Without your own freedom, you'll show up with others as unsettled, judgmental, edgy, grasping, manipulative, and needy.

In that mode, you will forever give away the best parts of yourself. Desperately searching for answers from the wrong questions. Waiting for something or someone to come along and magically grant you permission to finally start living your own life.

By not granting *yourself* permission to embark on the Freedom Adventure, think of the risks you're assuming:

- No organization, community, team, lover, child, or friend will fully trust, respect, or want the company of people who, in the moment of truth, flip-flop on their word or fail to live by their own professed beliefs or convictions.

- No audience will line up, be captivated by, or rise in ovation to people afraid of their own voices or uncertain of the platforms on which they stand.

- No fan wants to follow athletes, artists, or performers, no matter how gifted, who strive to be seen above all others, chasing personal gain, leaving hot messes in their wakes.

- No customer wants to line up or pay money for business propositions, no matter how enticing, built on values that wither under the weight of fear or greed.

- No children want to see their parents as weak-willed, dependent, or easily manipulated.

- No consenting adults want to fully share or surrender their sexuality with partners who don't love, trust, and care for their own sexuality.

Have you given yourself permission to think, feel, and act freely? Would you know the difference?

Without realizing your own independence, no matter how hard you work, how much you accumulate, how well you provide for your family, how good a parent, partner, friend, lover you try to be, you'll always be longing for something more.

Not taking the Freedom Adventure means passing all your own limitations, fears, and anxieties straight down the line.

Mother, fathers, and caretakers of all kinds, pay attention. Perhaps this is the ultimate price of not undertaking your own Freedom Adventure:

Our repressed, unresolved shit has a way of seeping out and mucking up life for everyone and everything around us.

Sure, it can feel like a huge risk to address your own baggage head-on. To sport the "work-in-progress" T-shirt. To put the not-quite-perfect version of yourself out into the world. But keeping your real truth buried burns vast amounts of emotional energy and comes with far greater risk. It's literally a form of orchestrating your own "dis-ease" across your biggest life priorities and pursuits.

Work and career. You'll see possibility in the distance but never quite reach the shores of maximum impact and fulfillment. You'll stay stuck in mediocrity, playing it safe (and small), repeating the same roles and patterns, watching the successes of others from the sidelines with frustrated envy.

Money. You'll be driven by scarcity and accumulation, afraid to lose what you've built up. You'll recycle regret over property you didn't buy, the stock you didn't sell, the big move you missed…forever chasing financial security through more, more, more.

But "more" never brings peace. No matter your starting point or amount of wealth accumulated, "financial security" will remain a distant apparition.

Relationship intimacy and sex. You'll bury the essence of your natural compassion, the full capacity of your big-hearted humanity, and, with them, your powerful gifts of touch, tenderness, affection, and intuitive understanding.

Your sexual urges will manipulate your mindset and lead to unhealthy behaviors and unrealistic expectations, imposed on yourself and on others. You will end up dousing the flames of your own fire by being overly nice or compliant, underplaying your genuine appeal to avoid rejection (a guaranteed intimacy killer). Or, you will succumb to the rut of transactional performing, denying your partner and yourself the exquisitely delicious experience of intimacy—open, honest, and trust-based giving and receiving.

And if doubting your own desirability isn't obstacle enough, you will fall into the trap of expecting your partner to do the work for you. To love you in ways you don't yet feel free to love yourself.

Living an imitation of truth is never sustainable.
When pretending, when faking,
eventually cracks appear. The dam breaks.
A reckoning is inevitable.

Over time, like any hurt left untended, things fester for the worse. And, when the toxicity leaks and ultimately explodes, that noxious waste spills into the lives of the people around you. Your colleagues and friends. Your family, partner, and children.

As you stand at the base of the Freedom Adventure, you hold the power to redirect that kind of reckoning, discontinuing that cycle for yourself and generations to follow.

SO, WHAT LIES AHEAD ON THE FREEDOM ADVENTURE?

Here you are, at the start of the trail. Eager and energized. Ready for action and the adventure that awaits.

The Freedom Adventure is all about claiming independence. It's about deepening self-awareness and sharpening self-regulation. That entails arriving at a fresh perspective on where you've come from, all you've been through, and who you've become as a result. It requires you to release that which no longer serves your true nature and highest calling. Ultimately, it is about trusting your place in the world, in any situation, without carrying the weight of attachment, entitlement, or dependency.

On the Freedom Adventure, you will learn how to:

- Derive a more complete meaning from your past
- Master your strengths and fears
- Trust your mantra in life, breath to bone

Here's what you most need to know.

The Freedom Adventure is about discovering new meaning.

Of course you already "know" yourself, to a certain degree. This adventure delves into deeper territory than you've gone up until now. It starts by delving into the past to discover peace and strength. That requires going down-and-in to acknowledge the difficulties and honor the humanity of the people, places, stories, and situations that shaped you, without being directed or derailed by any of it.

The Freedom Adventure is about orchestrating natural endings.

It's about weaning off lingering childhood attachments, old stories, or outdated beliefs that have since been proven incomplete, if not outright false. It's about burning bridges that keep you thwarted or tempted to turn-tail, run back, or seek temporary (again false) relief from the fullness of your unique abilities and true potential.

It's about the noble celebration of death, literal or metaphorical. Gracefully and firmly bidding farewell to what *must* be left behind—a relationship, an identity, a belief—in order to make adequate space for what lies ahead. Organically beginning the discovery of fresh trails meant just for you.

That requires you to launch up-and-out, be reborn, worthy of creating and thriving in a life of your own. It's about moving forward, complete with who you are, proving nothing to anyone apart from yourself.

The Freedom Adventure is about mastering strengths and fears.

That includes honing expert knowledge of your unique abilities *and* their related fear counterparts, which together form the detours and dead-ends lingering in the background. Claiming your freedom is not about ridding yourself of fear, but about being *with* it, living *beyond* it, so you can approach the world with an independent, neutral stance (an absolute must-have to be successful on the Courage and Power Adventures ahead).

That requires you to first see, then befriend, your demons. Only then will you master the many dualities inside you—risk and reward, pain and joy, success and failure, facts and fiction—and know how each ingeniously informs your next important step forward.

The Freedom Adventure is about claiming a mantra for the one life you've been gifted.

It's easy to confuse the terms "purpose" and "mission." Many of us, especially when in team and organizational settings, use those words interchangeably. Rather than getting slowed down trying to distinguish between the two, for now let's agree that purpose and mission are both *service driven*. In other words, they both speak to what an individual or collective chooses to *do* with their freedom for the greater good, with others, through others, and for others—all important stuff, which lies just up ahead on the Courage Adventure.

For our purposes on the Freedom Adventure, think of a mantra as being individual and soul defined. In other words, a mantra is an accurate depiction (in a word, statement, or shape) of your extraordinary strengths and your principle perspectives and non-negotiables. The often unspoken code you live by every day, as if you were the only person on earth. In good times *and* in bad. When handy *and* when inconvenient. Your mantra is how you get clear and stay clear with yourself. What you want—as in *really* want—and why that is so important to you here, now, with the time available. What your boundaries are that guide what you are and are *not* willing to do in order to realize all of that.

Mantra is the final stage of the Freedom Adventure. It builds on the fresh meaning you have derived from your past and what you choose to carry forward with a noble sense of duty. It encapsulates your mastery of strengths and fears so you can be accountable for all you do and for the wake you leave behind. It's how you'll hold *tightly* to the life you want most and hold *loosely* to the exact path to get there. Your mantra serves as "true north" once you adventure into the many challenges ahead on the Courage Adventure.

> *Consider freedom your birthright:*
> *one part gift, one part duty, one part unsolvable*
> *mystery you'll return to time after time.*

Up until now, you've survived, maybe even thrived, on some form of answer to a few of life's many existential questions:

- How does my past shape the meaning of who I am now?

- What resulting skills, resources, and passions are mine to master?

- How do I lead myself forward, beyond fear?

Unless your answers are clear, succinct, and fresh, you're living today as if it's the past. Some important part of your professional, family, or personal world remains elusive, somehow "off," broken, or painful. Maybe seemingly beyond repair.

Why? Because at the risk of repeating the same points, without a fresh completion of the Freedom Adventure, your every move remains subject to a patchwork operating system that distracts and encumbers the most genuine version of yourself. You are likely:

- Chasing who you think you are supposed to be, according to someone else's definition, according to the influence of a parent (alive in your world today or perhaps already passed on) who is still pulling your strings.

- Buried by the weight of endless compromise and compliance, secretly wishing on something or someone to make it all go away. Envious of some imagined future in which you feel valued and validated.

- Burning precious energy scripting requirements, putting up conditions, or holding expectations for how everything and everyone should think, feel, and act, according to your specific needs—while simultaneously blocking the humanity in yourself and others.

That's why the Freedom Adventure comes first. In many ways I consider it the most important because it calls you to own your noble place in the world, first. And delegating that job to anyone else is foolhardy, as tempting as it may be to try.

Which is also why I believe the Freedom Adventure is the most liberating: it offers profound trust in yourself, leaving you complete and worthy, as you already are. Confident and capable, no longer consumed by fear or failure. With your authentic self on full display, your intuition and exceptional abilities become differentiating superpowers. You'll own the life you inhabit, with every person, situation, and decision you encounter.

In the pages ahead you'll get to practice navigating the arc of the Freedom Adventure, from those early disruptive sparks and emotional messes to the quick fixes and bold leaps forward. At each step you'll be invited to recalibrate your Axes of Adventure: balancing vision and presence to operate from the right altitude and balancing empathy and bravery to act with the right attitude.

Fair warning: like all adventures, don't expect a straight, smooth road. Remember, you are innately equipped with everything you really need. And if you get stuck, all the orientation covered in basecamp is just a few pages back.

THE FREEDOM ADVENTURE TRAIL GUIDE: WHAT WILL BE HARD AT FIRST AND HOW TO KEEP ADVANCING FORWARD

Recall the common and predictable arc all adventures follow:

- An initial, disruptive spark that excites your emotions and creates a mess
- Your critical-thinking mind grasping for control, offering an initial fix
- Expecting to stay stuck until engaging out of the box and trusting yourself to choose beyond that which you already know or have experienced to that point

> **GUIDE TIP:** The disruptive sparks you'll encounter on the Freedom Adventure are internal, meaning they come from within you. Remember, it's up to you: how you react emotionally, how long and hard your critical-thinking mind grasps for meaning, the amount of energy lost to fear detours and dead-ends, and how easily you open your creative-thinking mind to awakenings that allow you to choose a new path.

Here are some of the challenges you can expect and some tips on how to keep yourself steadily moving forward.

Early in the Freedom Adventure, you're going to confront shame.

Every family has secrets that threaten to disrupt the fantasy ideal. Who did what, when, how, and to whom. Shining light into old stories often reveals harsh judgments or silent enablement of family members and their flaws. Like in any game of broken telephone, these stories get passed on down the line, as if in an incessant undertow or perhaps a torrential tide.

Shame is born out of a belief that something about you, inside you, is permanently and inherently wrong. Left to their own devices, family secrets perpetuate exactly that: an underlying story that something about your family—and by extension of being born into it, something about *you* —is wrong. As if there's nothing you can do but accept a life of misery.

Even more damaging is the added burden of believing you're not supposed to talk about it. Most families talk around truths in code, hushing those who ask questions or start digging in the dirt about affairs, adoptions, entire second families, addictions and abuse, racism, betrayal, suicide, religious cover-ups, mysterious money trails, repressed or uninhibited sexuality...and the list goes on.

> **GUIDE TIP:** Think of your own typical family conversations about the past. The well-worn tales. Thin scabs barely formed over old sores. The inconvenient realities everyone works to avoid. The land mines that newcomers to the holiday dinner unwittingly step on (resulting in quick elbow jabs under the table). Think of how much easier, or safer, we believe it is to hang on to the old family "villain, victim, rescuer" stories.

In truth, carrying these sorts of interpretations into adult life cuts us off from seeing the humanity in our families of origin. In turn, the resulting blind spots repress and block us from seeing some of the essential humanity within ourselves.

Some adults aren't quite done blaming their childhood experiences on the imperfections of otherwise loving parents, who did the best they could while embroiled in their own struggles for freedom from inherited shame. Other adults are still subconsciously consumed by the actions of ambivalent, neglectful, or abusive parents or authority figures in their past —maybe even from generations ago.

With shame in the directors' chair we cast an entire plotline around the evil villain, hapless victim, and superhero, with ourselves in the leading role.

Without realizing it, we've shut down our access to freedom—freedom to see alternative paths, to detach from the stories of others, to choose our own ways forward, and to be accountable for the results we create and the regrets we allow to live on.

(Hmm, you might want to let that soak in, reflect, and write a few sentences in your logbook.)

After shame, you're going to confront guilt.

Whatever your family of origin, breaking away to discover and write your own story can initially feel like betrayal.

Wait, what?

Your first steps in the Freedom Adventure have you identifying the old childhood stories still tugging at your strings (or yanking your chain). Identifying what you were taught by mom, dad, and other influential adults about the meaning of home, family roles, work, money, sex, and so on. What often arises are actually *disempowering* stories, passed down through generations.

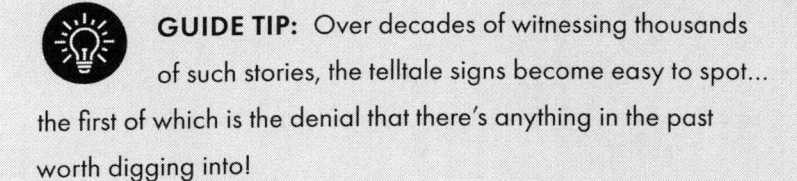

> **GUIDE TIP:** Over decades of witnessing thousands of such stories, the telltale signs become easy to spot... the first of which is the denial that there's anything in the past worth digging into!

So, be ready for it. As you move into the Freedom Adventure, some part of you, perhaps even some people around you, will want to keep you right where you've always been. Stuck in the same story, playing the same role, dancing to the same tune.

Expect resistance, as though you're somehow ungrateful, even disloyal. As if venturing out on your own equates to disrespecting those who came before you—even those who haven't done you any favors along the way.

Rest assured, that's all just old programming. Self-sabotaging, self-limiting bullshit.

Perhaps at a less dramatic level (or maybe not, depending on your family situation), breaking away from parts of your family story entails the same psychological hurdle as people who break away from cults. Charting your own direction forward invites waves of shame and guilt because it feels like you're doing something wrong.

Many of us also hit other waves of guilt simply by shining the spotlight on ourselves. Putting ourselves first can feel foreign. The Freedom Adventure is *all* and *only* about *you*. The price of admission is temporarily setting aside the many important "jobs" you have for others:

- As an individual, colleague, or with clients at work (the idea generator, the fixer, the boss…).

- In romantic partnerships and long-term relationships (the trip planner, the breadwinner, the bill-keeper…).

- As a parent (the bedtime story reader, the school liaison, the coach, the disciplinarian…).

- With extended family and friends (the host, the listener, the organizer, the caregiver…).

Don't worry too much. All those jobs will be ready and waiting as soon as your own work is done.

For now, acknowledge disruptive facts and process the emotional currents that rise up. Take some time to find mental meaning. Then, make the leap to freedom and resume life on *your* terms. Yes, you can both love your family of origin without taking on any lingering shame and guilt *and* love yourself.

Your first move forward is to slow down. That's going to feel frustrating.

I know, this is a terrifying prospect to any type A high achievers in our company.

But it's true. The first real step forward is to slow down, or stop altogether, all you've been so busily doing. In fact, you're not going to realize *anything* of lasting significance from the Freedom Adventure unless you first carve out capacity for the new by leaving *something* behind.

Some part of you isn't going to like that. Not one bit. Expect some old part of you to fight against all of this. That's okay. Just keep remembering:

- The entire world isn't actually resting on your shoulders. In other words, you're not actually that important in the grand scheme of things. If you haven't already, drop the self-appointed role of omnipotent overseer of what's best for everyone. (And if I still don't have your attention, stop taking yourself so fucking seriously!)

- Growth and achievement is all about steady momentum, no matter how small the steps. In other words, no more naval gazing, list making, or waiting for a better time. It's time to let go of any all-or-nothing, right-or-wrong impediments to action. Just get started.

- It's you who's in charge of you, and only you. In other words, you don't need anyone's permission or anyone's hands on the wheel of your progress.

- This day you're living in? It will never come around again. Even as you read this, a few more minutes just ticked off your remaining time on this planet. In other words, there is no better time to untie the knotted cords holding back your new beginning.

Get ready to feel lonely, or *lonelier*, at first.

I get it, you may be feeling lonely already, despite being surrounded by colleagues, friends, and family. You may be devoted to one or more of those detours and dead-ends, anything to avoid the initially daunting prospect of spending a single solitary moment alone in the vastness of your own freedom, the pure truth of who you are.

> *Consider this:*
> *the deepest form of loneliness*
> *stems from pretending to be something*
> *you are not, or are no longer.*

Why would anyone still hide the truth of who they are? Because they still equate vulnerability with weakness—the most self-harming, self-sabotaging falsehood we cling to when scared of losing control.

> **GUIDE TIP:** Performing some role other than the real version of yourself is exhausting. To "fake it" over any extended period of time—in a chosen profession, in a marriage, with friends and loved ones—creates serious inner turmoil. It's inevitable, sooner or later, that you'll alienate the people, places, and things you claim to hold dear. Or worse, you'll become lost to yourself. Stay on that path and one thing is certain: a reckoning is heading your way.

Overcoming loneliness is why I think of the Freedom Adventure as important *and* liberating: because authentic independence offers its own rewards. To be content in your own company, to be your own best friend and ally, is to never be lonely again.

Make no mistake, the Freedom Adventure takes guts. It's scary to stop pretending it's your job to be perfect, to satisfy other people's expectations, to carry someone else's load. To make the leap, you're going to have to shine fresh light on all your cunning and crafty ways of maintaining old pretenses. But spotting, then pinning down, that which is skilled at elusively operating in the dark is tricky work. You will have to out-fox the fox. Only then will you break through to the professional and personal thrills waiting for you. The big ideas you've been preparing for. The real experience of freedom you've been *longing* for.

Once on the Freedom Adventure your life
will become a whole lot lighter.

• • •

WARM-UP

As eager as we are to get started, let's not be those overzealous people who split their shorts by charging too fast out of the gates. We'll start with a simple warm-up. Nothing too involved, just some basics to get you started on the right foot.

> **GUIDE TIP:** When asked to take a deep breath, most people react like they're about to be forcibly submerged in water. I want you to feel how breathing in an evenly paced, full, and controlled manner is among the most freeing experiences you can do for yourself—anytime, anywhere, and it won't cost you a dime (in cash or crypto).
>
> If you have a tried-and-true breathing practice, go for it. If not, imagine (or watch) how freely a healthy infant or toddler breathes while resting peacefully: air inhaled through the nose, pulled in through the diaphragm; belly expanded, chest rising until full; an easy pause while full; a gradual exhale, air slowly plunging downward; belly contracted; an easy pause while empty; repeat.
>
> Take that image with you, since that's exactly how you were designed to breathe too!

Breathing your freedom.

Start by getting into a comfortable position. Shake out your limbs. Gently rotate your head, then neck and shoulders. Shift focus to your breathing, following this simple guide:

- **One.** Begin with a slow inhale through your nose. Feel your belly expand, lungs fill, and chest rise (like a round balloon, not a narrow tube) to a slow count. One…two…three…

- **Two.** Pause while full, at the top of your breath, for another slow count. One…two…three…

- **Three.** From your mouth, gradually exhale and plunge the air slowly downward. One…two…three…

- **Four.** Pause while empty, at the bottom, with nothing left to oppose your freedom. One…two…three…

As you breathe, let your mind wander while pondering the word "freedom." Take a moment to jot down a few related words or feelings that come up for you.

Here are some that come up for me:

- Words: *open, float, complete, effortless, timeless, vast*

- Feelings: *in tune and at home; trusting myself in my surroundings; bold exhilaration; clear, alert, and alive; victorious*

Next, try some free association. What personal memories do those words and feelings invoke? Write down a few recollections of your experiences with freedom. (Hint: Keep the focus on *yourself*. This is not about witnessing someone else's freedom.) Here are some memories that come top of mind for me:

- Coasting on a bicycle, arms raised to the sun-filled sky.

- Hearing the ball echo when shooting hoops alone in an empty gym.

- Turning in my resignation letter as CEO.

- Taking an impromptu vocal solo in the New Orleans museum of jazz.

- Starting the final marathon leg of a triathlon in the warm rain.

- Being swept away by Beethoven's interpretation of *"An die Freude"* in an oversold flight.

- Wordlessly inviting a packed auditorium to complete silence.

In those moments I knew who I was and trusted my place in the world. There was no past to relive and no future to anticipate; only full, sensory *freedom*.

* * *

STAGE 1:
Derive New Meaning from Your Past

Your first expedition is all about honoring family lineage and claiming your own noble place in the ancestral line.

Follow the flow of activities below, or use them to inspire a version of your own. Use your newfound technique to breathe into your freedom as you go. Utilize the full Axes of Adventure by tapping into your vision, empathy, presence, and bravery and follow each step through the Arc of Adventure that unfolds.

Remember, this is the first of three stages to your adventure with freedom. Be prepared to detach yourself from hoping, expecting, or requiring any other person to react in some specific way, just so you can feel good about yourself.

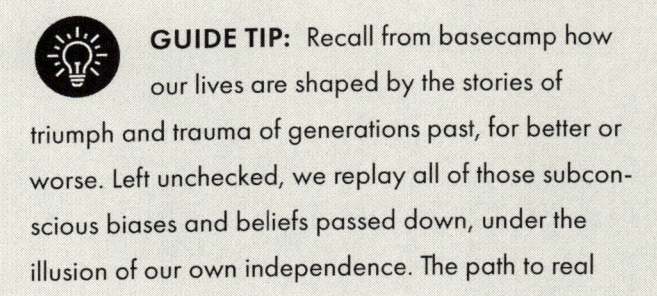

GUIDE TIP: Recall from basecamp how our lives are shaped by the stories of triumph and trauma of generations past, for better or worse. Left unchecked, we replay all of those subconscious biases and beliefs passed down, under the illusion of our own independence. The path to real

> authenticity begins by adventuring into your past and coming to terms with what you uncover.

Trace the family storyline that came before you.

Conduct your own primary research into your genealogy, as far back as you can go:

- Build your own family tree.

- Request biographical interviews with living family members. Put particular emphasis on your birth mother and father (first) and other influential caregivers from your childhood (second). Use relatives to fill in the blanks for those no longer with you.

- Resurrect pinnacle moments through family archives, photos, and keepsakes. Take notes and track your findings. Use video or audio to capture expressions, gestures, and voices. Safely store your written and digital logs for future reference, to be shared with those close to you and generations to come.

- Take a pilgrimage back to where you were born or to the places that influenced the lives of your parents and theirs.

Acknowledge how all individuals did their best with what they were given.

Beginning with your birth mother and father, note what is most meaningful to you. Organize your thoughts under three headings:

- **The Dignity I See.** For example, the highlights of the life your mother and father were born into. The burdens and gifts passed down. The challenges they faced. The coping mechanisms they developed. The strengths they drew from. The impact they left in their wakes.

- **The Forgiveness I Extend.** For example, forgiveness for the wounds and wrongdoings you have come to better understand. For the negative or painful impact you experienced directly and are now prepared to release, as it no longer serves you (and was never yours to begin with).

- **The Gifts I Receive.** The attributes, traits, or resources you willingly accept, carry forward, and blend into your own life. The source of your own unique superpowers. (Remember, if you're going to blame past generations for the bad stuff, you've got to credit them for the good stuff too.)

Personalize your completion and completeness.

Take an inventory of your discoveries in order to:

- Acknowledge and release any historical reference points that distort or distract your ability to see yourself as complete and worthy, as you are, right here, right now.

- Own your new narrative by writing out an accurate portrayal of the liberated and empowered person you are now because of all you've been through. This fresh version is undeterred by the opinions of others—void of proving, defending, or justifying a false image.

- Share this newfound meaning from your past with a parent or caregiver. Do so live, by requesting to meet in person; write your sentiments in a letter (that you may or may not choose to send); speak your words aloud at a place of deep personal meaning; or say them silently through meditation.

- Pass on what you have learned to your own children, close friends, and family, inviting them to find their own noble places in the family lineage.

> **STAGE 2:**
> **Master Your Strengths and Fears**

This second expedition is all about sharpening your understanding of fear, so you're able to live with it and mature beyond it.

Follow the flow of activities below, or use them to inspire a version of your own. Use your newfound technique to breathe into your freedom as you go. Utilize the full Axes of Adventure by tapping into your vision, empathy, presence, and bravery and follow each step through the Arc of Adventure that unfolds.

Remember, we never shed fear completely. You are here to get comfortable with your fears, as your freedom depends on learning to grow beyond them.

> **GUIDE TIP:** Recall from basecamp that fears are fictional stories we concoct, as this clever FEAR acronym reveals: False Evidence Appearing Real. Fear takes hold as you confront how little you actually know and control. On the adventure path, the whispers of fear offer tempting detours,

> which serve only to disconnect you from what you *do* actually know and control.

Name the story you're most afraid of.

Put pen to paper and complete the story:

- "I am afraid that if _____
  _____
  (fill in the scenario with names and/or situational details), then _____
  _____
  (fill in the negative result you imagine), and then _____
  _____
  (fill in the next negative result you imagine), and then _____
  _____."
  (Continue as necessary.)

- Write the *entire* fear story with all the specific scenery and players—the downward spiral of dominoes that you imagine will keep falling—until your fears are completely emptied out.

- Take your story to its ultimate conclusion: "And in the end, I will be _____."

Claim the origin of your fears.

Ask as you review your notes:

- What fears keep coming up?

- What parts of life are they most associated with? Work and career? Finances? Kids and parenting? Extended family? Marriage or romance? Body image? Health and well-being?

- Imagine peering down into a dark, dank well. What fears are at the very bottom? Are there one or two that overpower all others? What might they reveal about your relationship with money, work, status, or sex? Or how you identify with scarcity versus abundance, betrayal versus loyalty, feeling trapped versus autonomous, losing control versus taking a risk? Are you worried about making a mistake, being blamed, found out, or simply not being

  _____

  _____

  enough? (Special? Lovable? Daring? Worthy?)

- What feelings do those deeper fears invoke? Shame, guilt, anger, loneliness, or…?

Tame your fears with one of these tried-and-true hacks.

When fear comes calling, borrow from one of the FEAR acronyms I use to reframe the narrative away from factors *out* of my control and spur forward momentum toward factors *in* my control:

- A fear math equation: **F**acts + **E**motions = **A**ccelerated **R**esults (This is a reminder to get clear on which specific facts are triggering which specific emotions as the starting point to getting unstuck.)

- A cue before blindly following a fear detour: **F**urther **E**xplore **A**lternative **R**esponses (This is a reminder to spend equal time exploring the questions, "What else might happen? What else might be possible? And if *that* happened instead, then what, and then what…?"

- Or, if these don't speak to you, create a FEAR acronym of your own!

Imagine being in a movie director's chair (with your name on the back). Pick one of your fear stories and write the beginning, middle, and end. Then insert a new character, plot twist, or scene change. Write a few alternative endings in your very own "director's cut" to see which version you prefer.

On one side of blank paper, write all the things in your life today that leave you:

- Frustrated—discouraged, annoyed, blameful, enraged …(as many as you can)

- Envious—jealous, grudging, spiteful…(get them all out)

- Avoidant—worried, impatient, apprehensive… (anything about the future)

- Ruminating—guilty, remorseful, resentful…(anything about the past)

Then write across the top, **"This is my life when I allow fear to grow in me."**

Flip the page over and on the other side write all of the:

- Facts that are most present and real—the ones most worthy of your attention.

- Emotions you would *like* to feel—the ones that express the full spectrum of who you are and what it means to feel fully alive, now.

- Actions or adaptations that, if put in place, would lead directly to realizing those emotions—the forward steps *in* your control, drawn from what you already know.

- Results you really, *really* want to achieve, and all you imagine will be possible by releasing old stories and burdens that are no longer yours to bear.

Then write across the top, **"This is my life when I grow beyond the fear in me."**

> **STAGE 3:**
>
> **Trust Your Mantra in Life,**
>
> **Breath to Bone**

This last expedition on the Freedom Adventure is all about creating a mantra that defines your essence in how you relate to the world and in what gifts you offer each and every day.

Follow the flow of activities below, or use them to inspire a version of your own. Use your newfound technique to breathe into your freedom as you go. Utilize the full Axes of Adventure by tapping into your vision, empathy, presence, and bravery and follow each step through the Arc of Adventure that unfolds.

Remember, mantra is "soul defined" and all about how you live, as if you were the only person on earth. Keep that distinct from the "service-defined" notions of mission and purpose. (Those await on the Courage Adventure once you know the version of newfound freedom you are ready to show the world.)

> **GUIDE TIP:** The mantra you'll create captures the best, most authentic version of who you've become, how you show up, and the impact you leave behind. It's derived from exploring the meaning of your past and claiming the unique attributes you now carry forward with pride, honor, and nobility. It's the lens through which you tame fear and navigate uncertainty.

Go for a walk.

Find what you consider to be a calm, soothing venue for an outdoor solo walk. As you venture along, open all senses to your surroundings:

- What do you hear, smell, and see?
- What are you drawn to touch, or even taste?

Notice what beings, objects, or images capture your attention:

- A stream, the wind, a cloud. The sun, rain, or the moon. Morning dew on grass or a fresh patch of dirt.
- A fox, a scarlet tanager, or bumblebee. A popsicle or wild berry. An artistically foamed cappuccino.

- A bridge, crosswalk, or towering skyscraper.
- A soccer ball, jungle gym, or scooter.
  Abstract graffiti.

Keep noticing which one keeps coming back into your psyche. Tune in to that particulate being, object, or image. Get curious and start noting:

- How many of its positive attributes can you think of? What distinguishing qualities does it possess? Which are you most drawn to?

- How did it come into being? Why does it exist? What principles govern its interactions? Where does it get its energy from, and how does it recharge? What drains its energy?

- What are its essential superpowers? Under what conditions are those most on display?

- What are the benefits to its surroundings or to those who experience its most unique gifts? How does it leave its mark in the world?

Draft your story.

At the top of a blank page, write, "I am a _____." (Insert your thing, object, or image—let's start referring to this as your symbol.)

Use the same questions above to begin writing *your* story from the perspective of that symbol. Stay in the first person:

- My most appealing and distinguishing qualities are...
- I came into being by...
- I exist in order to...
- I get my energy from...
- I drain my energy by...
- My essential superpowers are...
- and so on.

In the days that follow, keep reflecting on your story. Say it aloud. Pay particular attention to which words convey the right energy, and remove the rest. Edit and refine it until it starts to roll off your tongue—succinct, clear, and authentic.

Claim your mantra.

Once you've landed on a story that captures the best in you, boil it down to a single sentence or statement. I've had several versions over the years and here's a recent one:

I am an Oracle.
 I see around, into, through, and beyond, always inviting adventure.

Try finding a graphical representation or design a logo that captures your mantra. Put a copy on your desk or in your journal. Better still, create a personalized screen saver, coffee mug, or baseball hat.

Breathe life into your mantra by repeating it as you start or end your day. Say it aloud before the big meeting, conversation, or event. Play it back in your mind as you transition between activities. Feel it in your body.

CONCLUSION:
Your Rite of Passage

Congratulations! You've completed each expedition on the Freedom Adventure to claim your independence. You know who you are and have earned the right to say:

🚩 *I belong to this moment, and it to me. I am ready to join forces with the world:*

- ☑ By deriving new meaning from my past I emerge complete
- ☑ By mastering my strengths and fears I emerge capable
- ☑ By trusting my mantra in life, breath to bone I emerge clear

> **GUIDE TIP:** Try saying these personal testaments aloud—or out LOUD! If they don't yet ring true, be honest and return to any unfinished business with the Freedom Adventure before recklessly forging on.
>
> Just remember, it's possible to spin your wheels in the Freedom Adventure, transfixed in some form of endless soul searching (aka eternal naval gazing). Be mindful of waiting too long for that exact right moment to get yourself back in the game. Remember, there's no such thing as "the perfect pitch" without a prepared

> batter who stands willing to take a swing at the plate (knowing a hit rate of three in ten is enough for a hall of fame career!).

Celebrate the milestone!

A traditional rite of passage follows a significant challenge that has been endured and overcome. We use such rites to mark a new status or identity and to usher in the next chapter of life. They also serve as constant reminders of how far we've come and halt any possible slide backward.

As the Freedom Adventure is akin to metaphorical death and rebirth, give some thought as to what you are ready to leave behind and how to symbolize who you are now in a unique and meaningful way. Here are some ideas to get you started:

- Declutter your life by bidding a fond (and final) farewell to anything that no longer serves your forward momentum. Wardrobe items, trinkets, and jewelry. Old photos and frames. Books and journals. Unused items in the cupboards or refrigerator. Club memberships, subscriptions, and social attachments. Any and all associations with the life you are now free to leave behind.

- Avoid "gifting" your clutter to family and friends. Make clean and anonymous donations to charitable causes. Or get primal and conduct a burning ceremony. Toast your past in a blaze of glory, ashes to ashes, dust to dust. (Be safe and responsible with this one, fellow adventurer.)

- Commemorate your freedom with an original design or symbol that captures the energy inside you. Commission a one-of-a-kind piece of jewelry or tattoo that says it all. Research the animal that embodies the spirit with which you will lead the next chapter of your life.

Some examples of freedom rites of passage from my own playbook include:

- Designing a custom tattoo to commemorate the completion of a big athletic achievement and self-determination milestone, blending images, colors, words, and numbers to express authentic meaning.

- Claiming the fox totem as my spirt animal and weaving personal imagery and metaphor into new professional branding.

- Conducting a fire ceremony to dispose of old papers and records following a major life transition and redefinition of home (complete with fire-inspired food, drink, and music).

* * *

You've done your independent work and discovered
the joys of newfound freedom.

Now it's time to step into the world of
interdependent relationships.

But your definition of courage is incomplete.

Until now.

CHAPTER 5

Welcome to the Courage Adventure!

Imagine that upon completing the Freedom Adventure, you were whisked off to partake in an extended launch party with your closest companions. A party which commemorated the closing of one major life chapter and celebrated the opening to the next. At the helm, ready to author the *attainment* of what to this point only existed in your imagination, this time your efforts are elevated beyond comprehension through generous exchange and symbiotic connection with all manner of people, places, and things around you.

The Freedom Adventure taught us to value authentic independence: deriving meaning from the past, mastering natural strengths and fears, and creating a mantra to trust and illuminate the way forward. All that work equips us for the world of relationships—the joining of two of more diverse and equally "free" forces to pursue a common vision or reason for being that neither can fully realize without the other. Relationships involve the fine art of mingling *in*dependence with *inter*dependence.

The Courage Adventure is the path to collective prosperity. It's where we get to show our newfound freedom—the best of ourselves—by collaborating, teaming, and partnering with the world around us while respecting the freedoms of all. Where we radiate possibility and prosperity, for all those around us to soak in, reciprocate, and spread further. Visioning, building, flourishing *beyond* anything we could conceive, let alone achieve on our own.

Investing in secure relationships of interdependence will take every part of your life to new heights. Here are some of the joys and payoffs you can look forward to.

COURAGEOUS PEOPLE FORM POWERFUL TRIBES, NATURALLY

On the Freedom Adventure, we learned that authenticity acts like a beacon, magnetically attracting like-minded, big-hearted, and soul-centered others. This notion is compounded in the Courage Adventure.

Being courageous starts by *living* our freedom. In so doing, we find ourselves in the company of those who live theirs. We know what to look for and are able to find courageous beings everywhere—often hiding in plain sight—whom we pass with a knowing nod. Some we follow from a distance. A select few will share our passions, connect to our aspirations, and be ready to contribute their own extraordinary talents toward the cause. We find ourselves invited to team with local communities, virtual networks, and global associations. We invest in the currency of premium relationships and trade on the synergies of mutual benefit, belonging, and trust.

This requires commitment to relationships of high integrity: those in which both sides clearly say what they will (and won't) do, before cleanly going about the business of *doing* what was said. And, when that doesn't happen, or if for some reason *cannot* happen as committed, we immediately offer options to repair what has been broken. We act to ensure relationship integrity remains intact, and often our restorative efforts render the relationship strengthened.

Alternatively, when relationship integrity is under threat of dissolving or has transgressed beyond repair, we waste no time. We don't placate or blame. We respect the individual freedoms of all parties too much to lose ourselves convincing and cajoling. We pause long enough to take stock, acknowledge the conditions which must no longer be tolerated (often exasperated by our own backslide from freedom or courage), and break clean.

> *Courageous beings don't linger in relationship vacuums once the other side has moved on. As one door closes, we open another.*

We also appreciate that not all partnerships, teams, or tribes are meant to be, or be forever. When a relationship reaches a natural ending, we courageously move on. Should any party resist (or persist) in upholding agreed-upon relationship norms, we defend what is most sacred. Freedom. Dignity. Basic human rights. For ourselves and others. We know what's most worth living for and fighting for. In voice or silence, through action or inaction, we know how to say no to guard the yes of what matters most.

If suitably provoked, we can also be formidable. In the face of weaker beings who use their resources to subvert basic human decency, those who would use their power *over* others, we are considered, swift, and exacting. We channel anger. Not in an unpredictable, unruly, or chaotic way. Not by punching down, impulsive revenge, or passive aggressiveness, but through our disciplined measure of control.

COURAGEOUS SOULS ARE SENSORY ARTISTS

We see more, hear more, feel more, sense more, and create more (all by talking less). We differentiate between what we *want* to see, or *expect* to see, and hold space for deeper insight to reveal itself. At our best, it's like seeing the world through 3-D glasses. Nuanced patterns come to the surface; colors are more vibrant; and we perceive the layers beneath, patiently waiting to be seen.

We know how to listen for more than just openings to resume our agendas. Our radar picks up pitch, tone, and emotional undercurrents. Rather than fixate on spoken words, we pay attention to body language and detect what is *really* being expressed.

We suppress our impulses to talk, and we confidently hold silence. We value the open space between stimulus and response, between any action and our reaction. We know how to use quiet stillness as an effectual teacher and a potent communication tool.

> *Courageous beings love to play.*
> *We are expert strategists, creative problem solvers.*
> *We are cunning and collaborative competitors.*

By extending these notions to how we touch, feel, and taste, we unlock our sensory artistry. Our appreciation of contrast makes us comfortable in light and dark, in pain and grief, and in the sensory delights of mind, body, and soul. We craft concepts, language, music, and physical forms to depict the complexities of life so others too may experience those same connections, in ways they're unable to reach on their own.

Our creative fire fuels us. With innovation. Resourcefulness. Resolve. Always finding a way forward. We are in a perpetual state of dynamic play with the people, places, and things that surround us. We take pride and pleasure in enduring hardship, in surmounting adversity, and in forging deeper relationships when pursuing meaningful work and honing our crafts.

COURAGE ALLOWS US TO THRIVE ON FEEDBACK

Courage allows us to hold even our sharpest instincts and longest-held beliefs as incomplete, leading to fewer blind spots. We drop our ego defenses when soliciting reactions without over-personalizing or condemning the sources, so we avoid getting swept up in flattery or beaten down by criticism.

All feedback serves as a multifaceted mirror we apply to test assumptions and appreciate how others experience us. This allows us to close any gap between intention and actual impact. Further, we stay tuned to lapses in self-regulation, when our emotional reactions are not as balanced as we'd like to imagine.

By not filtering everything through the veiled curtain of our own projections, we hold ample space for others to have their own valid reactions *without being diverted, perplexed, or consumed by any of it.* From there we build the bridge to common, mutual understanding, so we aren't misunderstood, easily fooled, or derailed.

The committed practice of accepting multiple perspectives builds critical muscle memory, which is crucial as the stakes go up. When tensions rise, so does the temptation to see contrary positions as impermeable and roadblocks as impassable. Courage allows us to remain clear in the face of discord and to channel conflict as the catalytic change agent it is—helping us to break through, to go beyond.

From that place of secure transparency, any offer, request, or acceptance of help is above the perception of weakness or frailty. Our radars scan for opportunities to reap and sow the rewards of engaging exceptional skills, perspectives, and attributes—from those in our inner circle or from complete strangers, with animals and nature, or in the material world. That might look like the perfect addition to the team. A guide dog or equine healer. A wearable technology to monitor vitals or enhance quality of life. The right prescription eyeglasses. A prosthetic hip.

> *Symbiotic relationships that respect and reciprocate interdependence liberate all parties to fulfill their essential missions in life.*

All of which helps us win more by failing smaller and learning faster.

The courage to not take ourselves so seriously means not feeling threatened about being wrong. We see mistakes as table stakes to growth, and we see failure as the most reliable method of informing our next courageous moves. The path to success is never a straight line. Like sailboats cutting into gale force winds, we set our sights on the horizon and tack our way there, testing, failing, and learning as we go. That kind of small failing is what preempts big failing. With each mistake, our experiences broaden and our wisdom deepens. Each misstep becomes a deliberate lesson that *need not be learned again*. In this way, courage is the surefire recipe to avoid living in regret and borrowing anxiety from the future. We live one day at a time, here and now, knowing the rest is an illusion.

THE RISKS OF NOT COMPLETING THE COURAGE ADVENTURE

*Without joining forces in relationships
forged in collective benefit...*

*your most extraordinary gifts will go unexpressed.
Your deepest passions will remain
just out of reach.*

*You'll never get your shot, manifest anything
of lasting meaning, taste exquisite pleasure,
or love so much it hurts.*

*You'll be forever on the outside looking in,
walled up, unfulfilled, and alone.*

WHAT DOES IT LOOK LIKE WHEN YOU ARE *NOT* LIVING WITH REAL COURAGE?

In a word: **manipulative** (of the passive or aggressive kind).

A lifetime entangled in needy coercion.

In the absence of courage, you will be blocked from seeing things in their most brilliant forms. Worse, you'll block the world from seeing *your* most brilliant form. Without acknowledging perspectives or possibilities that challenge your views (and comforts), you will remain blind to what those around you have to offer and ignorant to how things actually operate.

When you lack courage, the energy you devote to considering options and making decisions flows from two motivations:

- An attempt to control things (people, ideas, and situations) beyond your control

- An avoidance of things (people, ideas, situations) that invite growth

The compounding result is that your time, talents, and resources are consumed by manipulating people and situations for your own self-serving and self-limiting ends. Sometimes through strong-arm, bully tactics. Other times by subversive maneuvers or childlike games. Anything to avoid conflict or create a crisis. Anything to remain unchallenged or to divert attention from a truth you are still scared to face.

The world is full of such figures from past and present, in fiction and reality. They're easy to spot. You see them going job to job, relationship to relationship, project to project, complaining about how hard they have it, whining that no one appreciates them, and asserting dominance or silently sulking when things don't go their way. You know the kind of person I'm talking about:

The perpetual pleaser. The maligned martyr. The benevolent dictator. The boardroom bully. The rebel without a cause. The drama queen. The plagued perfectionist. The constant critic.

In real life, such characters always end up facing a reckoning, ultimately revealing their tragic weaknesses. And the closing chapters are never pretty: relationship roadkill, downward career spirals, squandered fortunes, dire health consequences, prison, and suicide.

> *Those without courage seek to ensnare others in their virtual merry-go-rounds of self-absorbed bullshit. Tragically, it's the only way they know how to deal with the emptiness in their lives.*

Here are some of the risks you face by not claiming your courage.

You'll drift from tribe to tribe, without ever belonging.

Lacking the fortitude to show your fiery passions, generous heart, and truest values, you won't attract courageous others. Being too timid to put your wants and desires out in the world, you'll also most certainly lack the confidence to ask for help. Nor will you spot opportunities to join forces, better yourself, or further your cause through the talents and resources of others.

Somewhere along the way you'll be invited into a tribe of potential peers, but you won't be asked to stay…because you'll still equate loyalty and trust with always holding the upper hand. Those with real courage will sniff out your inauthenticity sooner or later and move on without you. Your need for control to be right will attract only those too weak to create their own visions or stand for their own values. Underneath, you may even feel so threatened by the genuine courage in others that you'll find ways to rid your life of them, while holding them in jealous contempt.

Depleting courage is a slippery slope leading to one suffocating dead-end: a scarcity mindset.

At the core, scarcity equates to inadequacy. From that view, wealth is nothing more than an accumulation of assets. You'll be addicted to seeking and hoarding it, trying to satisfy an unquenchable thirst. No matter the size of your wallet, you'll never feel true prosperity. Everything will feel like a zero-sum game of winners and losers. You'll go out of your way to safeguard your stockpile and make certain to spread that philosophy to downward effect in other parts of your life:

- You will overweight your professional identity on title and status. You'll treat your work far more seriously than people will treat you.

- In family circles, you'll fail to see those around you, including your own adult children, as freely and fully capable of pursuing life on their own terms.

- You'll fail to foster meaningful friendships as you drift in and out of belonging—at work, with family, romantically. You'll be transient, without ever feeling truly at home anywhere.

- Spontaneous fun will seem frivolous and elude you. You'll never realize the kind of experience (while competing, enjoying nature, appreciating design, or connecting sexually) that blows your mind or opens your heart.

Locked in scarcity, you'll see everything as an expense, a personal tax levied just on you. You'll fail to see the disbursement of time, skills, and money as an investment in quality of life for the people and causes you care most about, where the return is immeasurable. Mistrusting, you'll penny-pinch, nit-pick, and complain everything is rigged against you, while begrudging those who invest in themselves. In the end, those with a fraction of your riches and resources will thrive in prosperous abundance, while that state remains elusive to you.

Cowardly people insist on living in the vacuum of their own echo chambers, repeatedly foiled by their own blind spots.

Witness the emergence of so-called "cancel culture"—the fanning of or gripping to extreme polarization in views, based in an unwillingness to appreciate context or seek source material. Of course, it's all pure diversion strategy. A last line of defense designed to resist an untimely truth, twist an inconvenient fact, or discredit a valid voice.

Do you find yourself surrounded by people who reliably agree with your position or consistently laugh at your jokes? Have you come to prefer the blather of your own voice? Are you stuck in the spin cycle of image management? If any of these resonate, you've managed to barricade yourself from any form of courageous truth. This backfires badly in three ways:

- First, within every voice of opposition, even coming from your staunchest rival, lies a vein of golden insight. But you'll never tap into that learning thread.

- Second, those you *really* want in your corner, who possess precisely the sort of insight, wisdom, empathy, and grit you'd benefit *most* from, will grow tired of your inability to absorb what they have to offer and move on.

- Third, those who remain with you in the end, perhaps only because of *their* lack of courage, will follow out of fear and revert to nodding in agreement simply to avoid the wrath of your blustering defensiveness.

If any of this sounds familiar, you are quite possibly holding a one-way ticket to a disastrous reckoning. With no one to hold the mirror and your refusal to look in it honestly, you'll soon be stuck spinning in your own feedback loop. You'll replay your own highlight reel and believe your own press releases. You'll fill the air with your own bullshit, seeing only that which validates your glorified grandeur.

Unable to claim your own boundaries, you'll bitterly resent (and secretly envy) those who courageously guard their own.

Lacking the fortitude to hold your own line, you'll constantly compromise your own important priorities. Any pretense of real courage will cave to the whims and wants of others, all under the guise of "doing what's best," a surefire path to your own victim narrative. Over-serving, over-pleasing, and over-helping all raise the stakes in your own martyrdom. Pretty soon, you'll find yourself getting walked all over, while begrudging those who hold their ground.

Without boundaries, your own negotiation strategies will turn against you. You'll continually box yourself in, never seeing the courage moves on the board in front of you. You'll never *quite* get what you want, or it will seem that the other side got the better deal. Ironically, you'll be so caught up in your own emotional and mental gyrations that you'll miss what's actually happening with the other side. In the end, you'll wind up negotiating really only with yourself!

Ultimately, without the Courage Adventure, you'll become sidelined. Fast.

Continually playing to your own lack of courage is like doing one type of exercise over and over. You develop the muscle memory of playing overly cautiously, fearfully, and small until it becomes strong and dominant.

Unfortunately, that leaves you decidedly unadventurous, albeit extremely well-prepared to sidestep and endure unpleasant, painful, or harmful situations that might have been resolved long ago. It invites colleagues, family, and romantic partners to walk all over you or take you for granted. It tunes out your body's cry for attention, as you find reasons to tolerate weight gain, poor sleep, back and neck ache, migraines, joint pain, skin conditions, temperamental moods, low energy, and so on.

You'll be stuck in outdated routines, energy-draining pursuits, and dysfunctional relationships. You'll be the one who courageous people make clean breaks from, and you'll never know the difference.

Chronological age won't be the biggest accelerator of your demise. You'll lose your place day by day, living in a world of constant change without the benefit of diverse resources and relationships in your corner. Simply put, you'll never grow beyond what "used to be" while the world moves ahead without you.

Watch your success—professionally, romantically, personally—contract or expand in direct correlation to the courage you are embodying.

SO, WHAT LIES AHEAD ON THE COURAGE ADVENTURE?

The Freedom Adventure was all about claiming and trusting your authentic independence. You've emerged reborn: complete, capable, and clear. Now your newfound freedom is ready for primetime.

The Courage Adventure is all about joining forces with the world to invite mutual benefit and realize collective advantage. It's about enjoying a level of prosperity beyond anything you (or any one person) is capable of alone. It's about experiencing all that symbiotic, 1+1=3 stuff at work, at home, at play, each and every day, which requires a relationship approach based on clear communication, reciprocal respect, and a shared commitment to interdependence.

On the Courage Adventure, you will learn how to:

- See and savor the essence of life around you: the beauty and flaws and the inherent dignity in every work in progress.

- Accept and acknowledge differences, above any need to control. Appreciate the stage of maturity and readiness for change. Understand the support to offer and the boundaries to respect.

- Best engage and thrive with others. Respect individual agency to ask for and accept the help needed most. Operate under clear terms of mutual advantage and adhere to norms that serve all sentient beings. Cleanly part ways when it's time to move on.

Here's what you most need to know.

The Courage Adventure begins with self-disclosure.

Think of this as your first step toward putting your newfound freedom to the test. Trusting yourself enough to reveal all of who you are *now* is the price of admission. No more hiding or deploying distractions. That's why the Courage Adventure is so challenging; it puts everything from your adventure with freedom to the real-world test. Are you ready to *live* it?

That requires you to drop the mask (or full-body armor!) that used to hide insecurity. Instead, by unleashing the next complete, capable, and clear version of yourself, you get to arrive securely in any situation, without requirements or needing to know the outcome before taking a risk.

Courage is living your freedom, fully engaging in the world, with equal parts confidence, grace, and humility.

The Courage Adventure is about discovering and dignifying differences.

The Courage Adventure invites you to suspend everything you *think* you know about the world and how it works to allow for curious interrogation and humble reflection. To see, hear, touch, smell, and taste the essence of all things, as if for the first time. To gather feedback that challenges, disrupts, dismantles, and *disintegrates* your prior experience bias about what "is" or what "must be true."

Along the way, you'll discover gaps in understanding and grant others the dignity of being different, just as the Freedom Adventure taught you to honor unique facets in yourself. As you pry apart your old instincts and lay bare more insights for consideration, you'll begin to rebuild and *reintegrate* a more expansive, more evolved view of the world, of everyone and everything in it, that incorporates new facts and possibilities.

The Courage Adventure frees you from a false sense of control. It fosters acceptance of all that is beyond your control, leaving you to control the only thing you can...you.

Do you see the world around you honestly, gracefully, objectively, and accurately? Are you able to move beyond mere tolerance toward accepting and appreciating the differences you see? Can you voice your perceptions in a way that the "other" in your purview feels truly *seen?* Seen as worthy, unique, and capable—as *free* as you've come to see yourself?

All of this is actually about accepting and acknowledging just how much of the world, along with everyone and everything in it, works in ways completely and utterly beyond your control.

> *Boil it right down.*
> *The only thing you control in absolute*
> *are the thoughts you choose in anticipation*
> *or response to any condition*
> *or circumstance.*

When combined with the skillful self-awareness and impulse regulation you acquired on the Freedom Adventure, the Courage Adventure teaches you *real* control. The kind that comes only through being an agent of your own response. Only then will you unlock the depth of courage required in any given moment to:

- Meet the world where it is, as it is.
- Greet others where they are, as they are.
- Choose to be the best of who you are, in any moment.

Will you admit your own limitations? Out loud? Are you able to honor conflict, see both sides, and even celebrate the full spectrum of equally true perspectives before rushing to form a polarizing conclusion?

You'll learn to see through a lens of abundance and choose your way forward from there. That requires you to release the pull to interfere, manipulate, cajole, grasp, force, or otherwise abandon your newly claimed freedom in a rush back to satisfy some old dependency or latent insecurity.

The Courage Adventure asserts your agency to create and maintain healthy boundaries in secure, *inter*dependent relationships and simply detach from all the rest.

Not everyone and everything is going to fit where you are now, what you most want, and what you're prepared to do to go after it. Some won't share your altitude of possibility or attitude of readiness. Others won't have the skills now, or maybe ever. And to be sure, others are already *way* ahead of where you aspire to be.

The real question is whether or not you have the courage to concentrate on the select few, who, like you, have come to earn and cherish their own freedom so that together you are able to pursue mutual advantage and lasting prosperity through *collective* security.

Then, it's game on. Enjoy complementary combinations with equal ability to negotiate the nuanced boundaries required for successful collaboration; to join forces and activate synergies on missions of shared respect and mutual advantage; and to pursue, create, and thrive beyond anything you, or anyone, is capable of alone.

> **GUIDE TIP:** Again, trusting the intuition born of your newfound freedom is paramount. It increases your ability to articulate and hold boundaries that grant others the dignity of their own choices—including what may be their own unfinished business with the Freedom Adventure—and your ability to gracefully, quickly, and cleanly detach from relationships built on fear, neediness, and other forms of insecure dependency.

The Courage Adventure is about your relationship approach with all sentient beings and material things.

Even if you have decided to live in complete isolation as a hermit on a remote island, survival still depends on courage. You still must build secure and interdependent relationships with forces beyond your control: the elements; native plants, insects, and animals; obstacles to securing shelter, food, and hydration; the difficulty of coming up with creative and meaningful outlets to pass the time. For the rest of us, we apply courage to our everyday interactions with all manner of people, living beings, places, and material things. Each interaction is an adventure waiting to happen.

On the Courage Adventure, you are challenged to offer the best in yourself as an investment in collective prosperity, not as an expense charged against your own account. That's why the payoffs are so rewarding; you get to put down the weight of doing it all and open yourself to feeling secure through and with others—professionally, with family and friends, and personally, when on your own. You get to succeed individually and collectively in your most important passions, priorities, and pursuits.

> **GUIDE TIP:** This Courage Adventure is **not** about always leading from the front. Sometimes you'll co-lead. Sometimes you'll need to get out of the way and follow. Either way, the Courage Adventure is about staying in your own lane. Leading yourself requires courage enough.

THE COURAGE ADVENTURE TRAIL GUIDE: WHAT WILL BE HARD AT FIRST AND HOW TO KEEP ADVANCING FORWARD

By now your familiarity with the Arc of Adventure will start feeling like second nature: spotting the disruptive spark, entering the mess of emotions, grasping for the quick fix, and choosing to leap into uncharted waters toward the thrills that await. As always, testing your effectiveness in moving from phase to phase is all part of raising your adventure game.

> **GUIDE TIP:** The disruptive sparks you experienced on the Freedom Adventure were primarily internally driven. Expect those on the Courage Adventure to arrive from external sources as you interact with people, places, and things operating independently, without your permission, beyond your control, and without regard for your personal plans. What may start as a common disruption is likely to excite different emotional reactions in each participant, different attempts to fix the mess, and so on. That added layer brings complexity to the same predictable adventure arc, which this time you'll traverse alone **and** together.

Here are some of the challenges you can expect ahead and a few guide tips to keep yourself steadily moving forward.

First, get ready to confront your own courage altitude and attitude. You may not be as well-oriented as you think.

Pop quiz, which requires only a few moments of reflection:

Do you still require people, places, and things to be a certain way solely to feel good about yourself?

If so, you've got unfinished business in the Freedom Adventure. At this point, you'd be smarter to go back for a refresh on letting go of your old tried-and-true preconceptions. Really, you might not yet be fully prepared to take on the challenge of the Courage Adventure at this time. And when you *are* willing to move beyond everything you think you know, beyond your sense of what's possible for you and the world ahead, then the Courage Adventure will be right here waiting.

Remember that suspending your preconditioning is the entry fee. You'll know you're on the right track if the early course terrain is disorienting. Stay with it, and go easy. Even if you're not thrilled with your current state of openness, treat it as simply a starting point. You've now got a "courage benchmark" on which to build. The faster you commit to the Courage Adventure, the sooner you'll look back with amazed amusement at your former self.

Next, you'll confront your still-maturing ability to see into the essence of things.

No, the art of seeing is not some mystical skill reserved only for spiritualists in flowing robes.

We're talking about building the habit of stopping long enough to notice more than your initial sensory impression. About pausing the pull to quickly collate data and form snap judgments. About resisting all those tricks we use to restore and defend our own monopolies on the truth.

The Courage Adventure practices the art of *adding* to your overall impression of the truth for the purpose of *expanding* what's possible for you and others. Your aim is to see beyond the surface and into the heart of the matter to reveal what is most real, timeless, true, beautiful, and even painful. To see the two sides of every coin. The yin and yang. The light and shadow in everyone and everything, if you're willing to see with courage.

Seeing with courage becomes possible once no longer preoccupied with getting the world to see you.

Trust me, real mutual and collective prosperity happens only when you drop your drive to be seen. Do that, and everything you *really* need to thrive in life has a way of just showing up.

Before you're done, expect to be tempted by an old desire to fix and repair the imperfections you see in others.

Fair warning, this part of the trail can be steep. It involves *truly* greeting others at the altitude and attitude of where they currently are and graciously gifting them the dignity of their past, present, and future choices. Easier said than done. Those acts require *real* courage.

> **GUIDE TIP:** Let that sink in. Courage means accepting that others are imperfect, make mistakes, and have their own limits. Just like you and me, everyone is in the midst of their own adventures with freedom, courage, and power. Right?

Not everybody's going to want what you want in any given moment. Expect others to say no, often. Your response is testament to how far you've adventured with freedom and courage and the work that remains for you ahead.

Finally, expect to discover the important distinction between tolerance and acceptance.

Landing on the square of tolerance denotes a sense of edge. A begrudging agreement you make with yourself to proceed with conditions that work against your true nature and threaten your detour from adventure. This is not what acceptance is about.

And don't confuse acceptance with resignation. Accepting does not mean condoning serious boundary violations. At no point on the Courage Adventure are you expected to throw your hands up in exhaustion and declare, "Okay, you win. I'll drop my own courage and succumb to your cowardice."

Instead, acceptance is about finding peace with the way things are, releasing blame, and maintaining sole responsibility for your own actions and outcomes. It's about learning to let things be. Staying in your own sphere of control, choosing to live by your own boundaries.

Similarly, acceptance becomes possible once no longer preoccupied with getting the world to accept you.

Make today the day you let everyone off the hook, starting with yourself.

• • •

WARM-UP

Recall how you learned to "breathe freedom" in four evenly paced steps by loading in positive associations with personally curated words, feelings, and memories. We're going to do a simple build on that. (If you want a refresher, go back to the breathing warm-up we did before the expedition stages of the Freedom Adventure.)

> **GUIDE TIP:** How many times do you breathe in a minute? The adult average is around twelve to eighteen. That number increases due to anxiety, fear, or tension with a predictable negative effect. Slower breathing enhances cerebral processing, calms the nervous system, reduces stress, improves athletic performance, aids sleep, and lowers blood pressure.
>
> To make it personal, imagine twelve breaths a minute over an entire day—or measure your own breaths per minute and load in the math:
>
> 12 breaths/minute = 720 breaths/hour
> = 17,280 breaths/day
> (including during sleep)
>
> The act of breathing slowly, especially in the face of uncertainty or fear, requires courage. Imagine the health, performance, and longevity benefits to being more conscious of how you use those 17,000+ breaths each and every day. Quite literally, investing in the quality of each breath has immediate and long-term correlation to the quality of your entire life.

Breathing your courage.

Recall that true courage is all about seeing beyond your own biases, accepting that which is beyond your control, and choosing how best to foster strong, symbiotic relationships that create a level of prosperity beyond anything you're capable of alone.

It's all possible. The trick is accessing courage when you need it most. That requires practice.

Your first and best winning move is to slow down your breathing as a practice, well ahead of those crucial moments of courageous truth. You can achieve this in two simple steps:

1. **Even out your timing.** Start with an even three-count at each of the four breathing steps: slow inhale through the nose, a pause at the "full" top, gradual exhale through the mouth, a pause at the "empty" bottom.

2. **Lengthen your timing.** Play around with gradually increasing your three-count, while keeping the count even throughout in order to raise overall breathing efficiency and gain the related benefits. If you were to work up to a five count at each of the four breathing steps, each total breath from start to finish becomes twenty seconds for a rate of three breaths per minute, far more efficient than the twelve-breaths-per-minute average. (You can do your own math if you want to be more precise).

The next key to harnessing the benefits of breathing courage is found in the stillness *between* breaths—in the lungs-full "top" and lungs-empty "bottom" parts of the breath. This is the timeless space between action and reaction when nothing has happened…yet. That precious pause allows you to check in with your emotional, mental, physical, and spiritual state; calm any overly excited parts of your nature; and reengage with your vision, presence, empathy, and bravery. Those are the courageous spaces in which you grow (or stagnate). That's where adventure lives.

Put down the book and give it a try. Even out your timing at each breathing step, lengthen the timing of each step, and pay attention to the stillness between breaths.

Play with building this courageous breathing practice into your daily routine. Perhaps upon waking each morning. Before getting in or out of the car. Ahead of the important meeting. After listening and before responding. As you line up the big shot or plan the bold move. And again, as you drift off to sleep each evening.

* * *

> **STAGE 1:**
> **See and Savor the Essence of Life Around You**

This first expedition on the Courage Adventure is all about learning to appreciate the essential freedom in everything and everyone around you.

Follow the flow of activities below or use them to inspire a version of your own. Use your newfound technique to breathe courage as you go. Utilize the full Axes of Adventure by tapping into your vision, empathy, presence, and bravery and follow each step through the Arc of Adventure that unfolds.

Remember, it takes real courage to deconstruct everything you think you know (or are supposed to know) about the world around you and to open your senses to absorb more of what's real, right here, right now.

> **GUIDE TIP:** Recall from basecamp that your bias distorts your perception of the world around you. You project what you want for yourself onto others and see only that which keeps you feeling safe and secure. With your freedom intact, you're now able to willingly suspend all prior

> convictions and tap the brakes on expecting, or even anticipating. Now you're able to see things in their own authentic, independent states.

Bring more intention to noticing the world around you.

This is a simple build on where you left off in the Freedom Adventure. As you go through the ups and downs of day-to-day life:

- Tune your senses into noticing more about the things, objects, and images around you. The ordinary and mundane. The awkward and astonishing.

- Begin to observe more about the people around you. Work colleagues and customers. Strangers and service workers. Close or distant friends and family members.

Start by seeing more and listening more.

Keep all senses open and alert as you interact with sentient beings in the natural world or inanimate objects. Let's agree that when observing other people, you will do more seeing and listening (and reserve the smelling, touching, and tasting for only those closest to you, with clear consent!). As you look around:

- See more of the environment—the situation, parameters, and variables in play; the facts, options, actions, and reactions; the hidden incentives and intentions; the actual impact, immediate and residual.

- Listen more by not taking things personally or making what you hear all about you. Whatever your motive, put away the desire to react or intercede. Pay less attention to exact words and more to tone, pitch, and resonance. What is the real sentiment being expressed? What isn't being said that's most worth paying attention to?

Play the part of an objective, impartial investigative journalist.

Apply the same baseline questions you asked yourself on the Freedom Adventure to the world around you. Just as you used these questions to better know yourself, use them to better discover the most fascinating, intriguing, authentic qualities in all you encounter throughout daily life.

Whatever your subject—person (a loved one, new co-worker, a relative stranger), a place (the city of Paris, a meadow, a restaurant), a being or object (a woodpecker, a piece of toast, the toaster)—slow yourself down and stay alert to when your bias, judgments, and expectations cloud your view. Note in your journal:

- What distinguishing qualities are most noticeable? How many positive attributes can you observe?

- How did these people, places, beings, or objects come to be here, now? What influences played a role in shaping their existence? What unique skills and strengths were developed as a result? What principles or perspectives govern how they relate to the world?

- Where do they get their energy from and how do they recharge? What drains their energy? What fears might linger behind the scenes? What would provoke those? What superpowers do you see? Under what conditions are those most on display? What are the benefits? What marks do they leave in the world?

- What are the common themes with your story or with the broader human story. Where do you sense elements of vision, presence, empathy, and bravery? What sources of inner tension and duality exist? Light *and* dark. Pleasure *and* pain. Loss *and* gain. Masculine *and* feminine traits.

Put your observational skills to the test by requesting the opportunity to reflect back what you've seen and heard, or share your opinions with another:

- How close are your affirmations? How far did you miss the mark?

- Do you have the courage to invite reciprocal observations? Is there a bigger opportunity to see more about each other, or perhaps just yourself?

> **STAGE 2:**
>
> **Accept and Acknowledge Differences**

This second expedition is all about the interdependent nature of all relationships and the ability to release any false sense of control.

Remember, real control begins with your depth of self-awareness and ability to self-regulate in anticipation or response to any condition or circumstance. That's a sign of true courage.

Follow the flow of activities below or use them to inspire a version of your own. Use your newfound technique to "breathe courage" as you go. Utilize the full Axes of Adventure by tapping into your vision, empathy, presence, and bravery and follow each step through the Arc of Adventure that unfolds.

> **GUIDE TIP:** Now that you've practiced seeing things in their authentic states and honoring the freedom in others (as you do for yourself), it's time to recognize your own role in relationships. Do you reject or accept relationships only according to your definitions of right and wrong, good and bad?

> It's time to wean yourself off any blatant or subtle attempts that keep you in the relationship driver seat, reconstruct your ability to meet the world as it is, and greet others where they are.

Expand how you think about being "in" relationship.

Consider that you exist in a perpetual state of relationship with the world around you. Beyond potential interactions with billions of other human beings, you are in relationship with:

- Other sentient beings—your dog Zöe, the hummingbird at your feeder, the rats in your garbage.

- The natural world—the roses (and dirt, grubs, and weeds) in your garden, the trees that clean the air you breathe, the water you drink, the food already in your system.

- Inanimate objects—the shirt on your back (or in your closet), the roof over your head, the book you're holding, that song you love (or can't get out of your head).

- Ideas and concepts—time, wealth, happiness, winning, losing…and the long list of others.

Gauge your level of acceptance in all relationships.

Draw a straight line to act as your continuum of acceptance. From left (no acceptance) to right (full acceptance), label five evenly spaced markers as so:

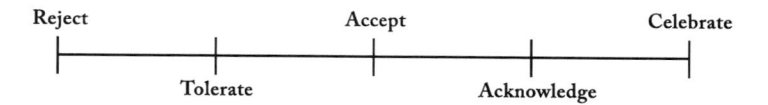

```
Reject              Accept              Celebrate
├─────────┬─────────┼─────────┬─────────┤
       Tolerate            Acknowledge
```

Pick the subject of any relationship currently captivating your attention. (Again, this could be a person, place, being, or object.) With your current perception, where do you gauge your side of that relationship is on the continuum?

- What factors led to your response? How does that position leave you feeling?

- What would cause your perception to move one way or the other? How might the other side answer?

- What does all of that suggest about your readiness to meet the other side where he/she/they/it is, with no judgment, personal bias, or other strings attached?

- What would it take for you to grant the same freedom to others as you honor in yourself?

- Are you able to gift the other side the consequences of their own thoughts, feelings, and actions, as a factor of being in their own perpetual state of adventure, a perfectly imperfect work in progress?

Stop holding others (and yourself) hostage.

Test the degree to which you have the courage to own your own stuff and leave others to own theirs.

Draw a simple two-by-two matrix labeled as so:

	Situations In My Control	Situations NOT In My Control
Choose to Devote My Time and Energy		
Choose NOT to Devote My Time and Energy		

- Select one quadrant at a time and imagine spending an entire week of your life activities bound by its parameters (e.g., Choose to Devote My Time and Energy/Situations In My Control). At the end of the week, how would you likely be left feeling?

- Now select a specific life situation that is consuming a lot of your time and energy. Map everything you are currently doing and not doing about it in the appropriate quadrant.

- What pattern do you see? If you shifted the time and energy you are devoting between quadrants, what then might be possible? For you? For others? For alternative outcomes or story endings?

(Hint: This might be the perfect time to brush up on the Serenity Prayer.)

> **STAGE 3:**
> **Choose How Best to Thrive in Relationships**

This last expedition on the Courage Adventure is all about asserting your agency to co-create symbiotic relationships that enable prosperity beyond any one person.

Follow the flow of activities below or use them to inspire a version of your own. Use your newfound technique to "breathe courage" as you go. Utilize the full Axes of Adventure by tapping into your vision, empathy, presence, and bravery and follow each step through the Arc of Adventure that unfolds.

Remember, through dedication to the shared adventure, trust deepens, relationships flourish, impact becomes evident, and change is realized.

> **GUIDE TIP:** In work and romance, with family and friends, as you interact in relationships of all kinds, you're building the foundation to negotiate mutually prosperous conditions that stimulate creative play and competitive collaboration without forcing or holding back. Now is the time to assimilate your heightened awareness and take meaningful

> action: to invite forward momentum and maximum collective gain. Prepare to welcome good fortune from unexpected sources.

At the heart of every effective communication is a courageous negotiation.

The Freedom Adventure honed your ability to communicate internally—to negotiate with yourself—first by claiming your own desires, then by committing to the cost of living out the pursuit of those desires on your terms. In other words, you are accountable for holding to the price of your well-earned independence. (And yes, you may still attempt to bargain for a better deal from time to time.)

You apply these same skills daily on the Courage Adventure. By sharing your independent desires and making clean requests, you invite the same in the world around you. From there, both sides may choose if, how, when, where, and why to proceed. (And you've learned now to expect a hot mess when that isn't the starting point for either side.)

Courage in a relationship means not taking things personally.

Not being afraid of conflict. Talking less and sensing more. Engaging in competitive, collaborative play. All these traits are what allow you to consider run-of-the-mill requests, or even outlandish flights of fancy. Whether in one-off transactions, during professional engagements, or over lifetime relationships, courage allows you to negotiate terms of *interdependence*, leading to mutual benefit and collective prosperity.

As the stakes rise, as emotions fire up, courage lets you withstand the heat, knowing when to parley, move to the same side of the table, or take pause. Try following this course as you imagine or prepare for an upcoming negotiation:

- Whether initiating or responding, start by getting clear on what is most important or worth solving for. You'll want to hold tightly to that and loosen your grip on exactly how to get there.

- Clarify agreements with the other party up front, such as setting parameters around confidentiality, avoiding distractions or interruptions, staying engaged for an allotted time, and requiring the parties to speak only for themselves (and not on behalf of others, present or absent).

- Use clean and succinct responses to any request—that will help keep the ball rolling. For example, begin with either a yes, maybe, or no:

    Yes, and here's how I would be willing to make that happen…

    Maybe, if you (or we) were to also…

No, but I would consider instead…

- Grant both sides the dignity of their own adventure arcs (the mess of emotional excitement, the mental grasp to fix using historical references, the choice to move ahead or stay blocked) as you explore and exchange tradeoffs that ultimately arrive at a mutually advantageous solution.

- Use the gift of silence to maintain open space for quiet contemplation and emotional reset. Trust your empathy and bravery to know when it's time to call a time-out, change course, or walk away. Natural consequences often offer the best, or only, conditions for genuine growth.

Start by getting clear with yourself in order to make clean requests of others.

For discussions that matter, invest a few minutes in sorting through your ideas, emotions, and proposals. Lead with sharp, succinct, and attention-grabbing headlines, as the details from the rest of the story may detract from your primary intention. Try following a simple script:

- What I most aspire to is…(tap your vision to state the BIG exciting prize and compelling future you imagine)

- That feels important to me now because…(tune your empathy inward to clarify and honor the top three emotions at the heart of your vision)

- The reality as I see it is…(use your presence to isolate the poignant few and irrefutable facts or most critical questions to explore and resolve)

- I am willing to let go of…I am *un*willing to let go of…and I am willing to step into…(engage your bravery to state and commit to your boundaries without hesitation or backsliding)

- Which leaves me wondering if you would be willing to…(now you are ready to make a clean request of others)

Write out your answers, say them aloud, or get objective feedback from an independent party. And before launching in, don't forget to offer the other side the opportunity to propose a time and place that allows them to commit their full attention.

Adventure onward to high-performance relationships between independent beings.

Whether in a team of two or twenty, or in an organization of twenty thousand, follow this roadmap to realize the sort of benefits, advantages, and lasting prosperity that is unattainable by you alone, or any one person:

- Start by asserting each individual's commitment to a clear and compelling vision, a desired future state empathetic to both heart and mind that inspires participation.

- Establish a unified understanding of the current situation, along with the focused beliefs and brave behaviors required for change.

- Acknowledge and celebrate the diversity of participants in background experience, skills and expertise, style and approach.

- Articulate individual role clarity and accountability, as well as the symbiotic alignment required between roles to eliminate overlap and fill gaps.

- Determine how information flows efficiently between parties, including the use of productive tension or conflict to ensure effective and timely decision-making.

- Establish methods to measure impact and create feedback loops that drive conscious adaptation as situations change.

- Build in regular periods to pause for honest reflection, recognition, and renewal.

CONCLUSION:
Your Rite of Passage

Congratulations! You've completed each expedition on the Courage Adventure and are ready to thrive in the world of relationship interdependence. You've shown the best of who you are and have earned the right to say:

🚩 *Through my relationships I create prosperity beyond anything I am capable of alone. I greet the world as it is, meet others where they are, and express myself fully as I:*

- ☑ See and savor the essence of life around me (beyond my old projections)

- ☑ Accept and acknowledge differences (releasing any need to control)

- ☑ Choose how best to thrive in the world of relationships (clear with myself and clean with others)

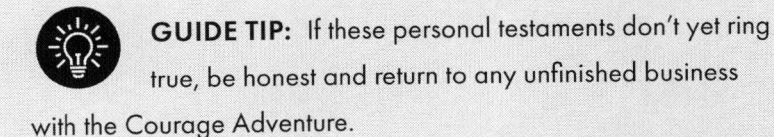

> 💡 **GUIDE TIP:** If these personal testaments don't yet ring true, be honest and return to any unfinished business with the Courage Adventure.

And a word of caution: believe it or not, it's possible to overstay your welcome in the Courage Adventure. No matter how good you've got it, over time things around you will normalize. Finding joy in simple pleasures, appreciating subtle splendors, will begin to fade. You'll hit a rut in day-to-day work and family interactions. You'll feel yourself captive to performing, numb to the same routine you and others have become accustomed to.

The familiarity will feel good, for a time. Some part of you will say, "I've made it," which is exactly when it becomes difficult to imagine your life without:

- The title and status (your professional identity and reputation)
- The lifestyle (your multitude of resources, excesses, and fingertip conveniences)
- The social network (the transactional, predictable posturing, just to keep the streak alive)
- The assumptions (that the people, places, and possessions in your life will all stay just the way you like them)

Beware, fellow adventurer. The more you pattern more-of-the-same, the more you dull your edge, dampen your flame, and lose your zest for life. When that voice inside whispers, "Is there more to life than this?" it's time to move on to the Power Adventure.

Celebrate the milestone!

As the Courage Adventure is akin to joining forces with other courageous beings and forces around you, give some thought in how to symbolize collaboration, alliance, or trusted bond in a manner meaningful to those who played a critical role. Here are some ideas to get you started:

- Embark on a celebratory trip or host a unique experience that reunites those involved. Share battle scars, learnings, and laughter.

- Co-design a symbol, logo, or memento that captures the collective consciousness. Plan a gifting ceremony that members may return to (or individual private acknowledgment of members) on special anniversaries to come.

- Make a charitable donation together. Plant a tree. Build a school. Reinvest your own prosperity in lasting ways.

Some examples of courage rites of passage from my own playbook include:

- Etching the initials of my sons' names in the final slab of wet concrete outside our newly built, collectively inspired family home. Returning to smile again years later.

- Hosting a live concert night with family and friends to celebrate a CD release (when such things existed) of original music written, performed, and recorded by our band of brothers.

- Mutually selecting a pair of soul-rings to celebrate individual uniqueness and collective courage after taking on all manner of personal challenge to reach the summit of relationship transformation.

- Collaborating with co-founders to create an evening of food, drink, music, and dancing to celebrate the one-year anniversary of a newly launched business venture.

* * *

You've joined forces with other courageous beings
to create and enjoy lasting prosperity.

Now it's time to revitalize, stoke your wildfire,
and celebrate the sanctity of life.

But your definition of power is incomplete.

Until now.

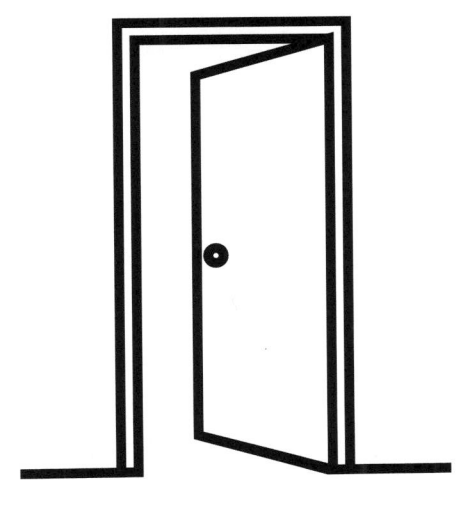

CHAPTER 6

Welcome to the Power Adventure!

Ideally, we would all be opening this page while in a place of personal pleasure—sipping a rich coffee blend at sunrise on a lakeside dock; perched in a mountain cabin watching the evening mist roll in; roused by undying beauty after leaving an art museum in a bustling world city center; cozied up in the comfort of home; anywhere, swept away listening to a transcendental piece of music.

Imagine whatever place that is for you. That's the energy I want you to feel. Stop. Take a deep breath. Look around.

You've achieved beyond anything you thought possible. You've worked hard to make it happen. Yes, seeing it all come together is incredibly rewarding, especially given some of the real challenges along the way. It's natural to want a pause button. To kick back, take stock, and feel proud of what it took to get here.

And for a time, we all do. And so will you.

(Or if you're still in the midst of striving and thriving with other courageous souls, stay the course. There may well be more juice left to be squeezed from the Courage Adventure before moving on!)

Expect some temptation to rest on your laurels and shift energy to protecting all the comforts you've built. But unless you have one foot in the grave and the other on a banana peel (and even then!), more adventures await, and you'll want to be ready. When you hear the half-brazen, half-terrified whisper, "So, is this all there is?" that's the Power Adventure summoning you to stop fucking around and seize the moment, while you can!

This adventure is about rejuvenating your power core. It's about being truly present with forces beyond comprehension and feeling them pulse through your veins. Living your own personal renaissance. Reawakening and stepping into it today. Knowing that afterward, things will never be the same.

The Power Adventure holds infinite payoffs and prizes. Here is some of what you can look forward to.

POWERFUL PEOPLE CHALLENGE THEIR OWN BOUNDARIES

Not for thrill-seeking or glory, but to celebrate the gift of living the fullness of their well-earned freedom and courage. Who comes to mind when you think of the most brilliant people you've ever encountered?

Those inspiring individuals who, regardless of the cards they were dealt, played each hand with mastery and grace. Whether living beings, historical figures, or fictional characters, they punched their tickets, rode lives of grand adventure, and the world was left better for it.

You were lucky enough to hear their stories, struggles, and triumphs. Perhaps you witnessed them in action or benefited from them directly in some lasting way. Maybe they planted seeds in you that bore fruit years later. Or provided the nudges required to tip you over the edge. Maybe they turned your whole world upside down.

Take a moment to jot down a few names of people like that for you.

As you consider those on your list, identify what primary power source they were most known for:

- Powerful in spirit? Artists. Writers. Dreamers. Inventors. Storytellers.

- Powerful in mind? Scholars. Truth Seekers. Scientists. Sages.

- Powerful in body? Athletes. Explorers. Trailblazers. Guardians. Warriors.

- Powerful in heart? Peacemakers. Humanitarians. Healers. Lovers.

Do you feel drawn to admire certain types of individuals or value certain power sources over others? (Hint: Your answer may reveal the one or two power sources most in need of your attention and renewal.)

Now imagine further those rare few whose influence and impact embodied *all* power sources. Those blessed with the uncanny ability to show up in any situation with just the right energy, delivered in just the right way, at just the right dose. Those able to channel mind, heart, body, and spirit with effortless agility, in a way that never feels inappropriate, forced, or constricted.

Somewhere these special souls caused you to make a mental note: "Wow, one day I'd love to try something like that."

Well, fellow adventurer, today is that day. Now is your chance to follow their leads by forging your own trail to live life on your terms, at your edge.

This is your wake-up call to challenge yourself intellectually, creatively, emotionally, physically, sexually, and spiritually. To test your limits and go beyond. Not for recognition, winning, reward, fame, approval, or status, but for the sole purpose of filling your tank with what it means to feel truly alive. To come face-to-face with all that is temporary, with your own impermanence, your own mortality.

> 💡 **GUIDE TIP:** Of course, leverage all the contacts and financial resources available to you but remember... we've reclaimed the definition of adventure from all those commercial stereotypes. We're on the hunt for the priceless experiences money can't buy. The Power Adventure is about growing through the meaning you'll make by stepping into the uncertain and unknown, equipped with all you've earned through the Freedom and Courage Adventures.

POWERFUL PEOPLE MAKE THINGS HAPPEN, HERE AND NOW

In any time or place, we know how to create the life we most want to inhabit, in each moment available:

- We acknowledge and own the countless choices that landed us in these precise places and times, without being haunted by resent or regret.

- With humility and gratitude, we appreciate how the cumulation of successes and failures prepared us for where we find ourselves.

- We believe there is some gift in even the most trivial of interactions—a treasure or invitation meant to be found, to move with, and to grow through.

- We picture a fortuitous future already unfolding, without worry or rush. We lead ourselves forward with open hearts.

Instead of burning energy reliving a past long since gone or borrowing yet unrealized joy or disappointment from the future, we keep growing as life unfolds, moment to moment. In this way of living, we keep our power flowing with maximum efficiency.

POWERFUL PEOPLE FLOW BETWEEN PAST, PRESENT, AND FUTURE

We either move with time, or we stop it altogether, for ourselves and with others. Most people operate in Chronos time, meaning the linear, steady tick-tock that marks the sequential passage of time. They track movements and activities using the clock and respect the time of others. (Or, if not, they have yet to complete the Freedom Adventure.)

The truly powerful also access Kairos time, meaning those nonlinear, surreal occasions when the clock seems to disappear. When the precise scene details, people, words, and feelings are so impactful that they become fused into memory, forever recallable at will. Not only do we realize when we are in such moments, but we can create them and invite others to experience these timeless moments for themselves.

We are adept at tuning out distractions of all kinds. Background noise. Food cravings. Needy people. Screen diversions. Pings and alerts. That level of sixth-sense presence allows our minds to absorb, retain, and process more. We know how important and rare that is in our world of near continual noise and commotion, and so we use it as a true differentiator when absorbing content, refining crafts, engaging with others, or engrossed in nature. We have access to the same 168 hours per week as the next person —it's just that we use that time more judiciously.

> *A higher order of power becomes possible when time is fluid and not over weighted to any past story, current reality, or potential possibility.*

GUIDE TIP: Flipping between time dimensions is a definitive characteristic of powerful people. They're never hurried or running late; nor do they overstay their welcome. It's uncanny how they seem to always be in the right place and time. Even decades later, they're able to tap right back into the most seminal moments and recall treasured sights, smells, and sounds as if they happened yesterday. Take careful note of such people when they cross your path—inquire about their relationship with time and borrow from their winning moves.

POWERFUL PEOPLE TRUST THE TRUTH OF THEIR UNFILTERED VOICES

They trust the truth that surrounds them, that came before, and in all that will follow once they're gone. This multilayered version of trust has three priceless benefits:

- We save ourselves from wasting precious energy circling back to relearn the same lessons again (and again).

- We grant ourselves permission to experience what is new, no matter how unfamiliar or daunting our environments.

- We have faith that what is needed most will be made available—perhaps not exactly in the forms we expect, but always in the way of highest needs.

In this way, our power becomes effortless when wielded with profound appreciation of the power around us.

As obstacle and opportunity merge, we trust our inner voice to ask for only what is most worthwhile, most obtainable, and most meant for us.

That's not to suggest that power equates to blind hope. Nonsense. We are assuredly optimistic, knowing how to ask the right questions that will bring forward the right answers, at the right time. That level of trust is contagious and penetrating to those around us. We sense safety in ways that we and others can rely on. We discern trustworthy faces, spaces, or places when we see them and have the ability to create them when we don't.

We listen and follow our inner voices with keen curiosity, allowing us to feel at home in any surroundings or circumstances, regardless of context, time, place, or role. We move toward, in, and through any mountains or gateways, with intention and purpose. We speak only when ready. We play only the notes that come from our souls.

> **GUIDE TIP:** Master-level power comes by extending trust to all living things that came before us, that exist around us, and that will live beyond us. We can feel all that power flow, permeate, and course through our veins. That kind of power captures the spirit of "ubuntu," loosely translated as "I am because we are"—where the royal we refers to *all* sentient beings that played a role in creating the current moment, and equally, *all* sentient beings whose trajectory will be forever altered by actions taken once the moment has passed.

POWERFUL PEOPLE ARE MENTALLY SAVVY AND EMOTIVELY EXPRESSIVE

We spot simple truths amid complex issues by leveraging all aspects of our mental capacities. Our critical-thinking analytical minds are alert to linear timelines, factual and binary analysis, risk mitigation, and problem solving. Our creative-thinking imaginative minds are open to nonlinear timelines, playful and nonbinary exploration, breakthrough visions, and out-of-the-box resourcefulness.

Honoring when and how to apply both sides of our powerful intellect allows us to see more of the truth from many different facets, without over-indexing on any one. We unlock the power of duality: that something might be this *and* that. We comprehend how the "whole" (of the person, place, thing, or situation) always includes something other than the sum of the parts we currently see.

*We know when the best path forward may require
the best of both sides to coexist.*

As a result, we express the intricate facets of what we observe more honestly, precisely, and accurately. Our broad emotional vocabulary intuits the essence of what is being stated or felt, individually or collectively. We make soulful, empathetic connections, extract meaning, and convey actuality—intense or challenging conversations, when viewing pieces of abstract art, during lovemaking, or when traversing mountain streams.

This is particularly valuable when managing our own blind spots. With Jedi-like self-awareness and self-regulation, we rise above *what* we are thinking to look down upon *why* we are thinking that way, *who* we are being as a result, and *how* that is likely to impact the situations we are in. From there our intuition plays out the chain reaction of events, empowering an ability to see a future *before* it unfolds and to choose an appropriate course.

POWERFUL PEOPLE NURTURE THE BRAIN WITH EQUAL PARTS STIMULATION AND RECOVERY

We are lifelong students and are continually making investments that keep our intellects supple and sharp. Formal courses and classes. Self-guided inquisition. Hands-on experiential learning. When we find we're the smartest people in the room, we know it's time to find a new room.

With equal importance, we know the power of the unfocused, wandering mind, and so we commit to recovery states, mentally, physically, and emotionally. We cherish open and unencumbered spaces. We savor silence and stillness. We are master-level daydreamers, walkers, and meditators. Our sleep is recuperative, allowing us to harness the power of dreams brought forth from our subconscious minds.

Powerful people utilize many strategies to ensure regular rest. We adhere to regular routines, utilize gatekeepers, create regular physical separation from our usual surroundings, and selectively apply technology as part of the solution.

POWERFUL PEOPLE ARE SOVEREIGN STEWARDS OF THEIR PHYSICAL BEINGS

We are lifetime athletes, outdoor activists, and nimble travelers. More than a temple, our bodies are phenomenal machines of genius design, capable of taking us anywhere we want to go; transmitting our desires, needs, and fears into action; and following our subconscious and conscious commands. We know there's no manual, refund, or trade-in policy—for better or worse, we've each been gifted exactly *unus corpus*.

Powerful people are dutiful, ritualistic caretakers of their physical beings. We listen to our bodies' desire for moderation and invest in knowing what keeps our machinery ticking. We make physical well-being a lifetime priority with nourishing nutrition and hydration; frequent motion and mobility; core strength and sensible weight-bearing exercise; and regular rest, medicine, and maintenance.

*We honor health as our first, last,
and greatest wealth.*

We use and enjoy our bodies. To create and bring our ideas to life. To compete with others, with nature, and mostly with ourselves. And as we age, experience accidents or illnesses, and our bodies decline, we forge on. We live big with every ounce of the physicality we have left, not bemoaning from the sidelines how our bodies no longer operate as they did decades ago and complaining they have let us down.

We conserve our physical energy and are deliberate in our gestures. Our walks are confident and measured. We don't flail our arms or move erratically. People notice the way we stand to acknowledge their entrance, and again as they leave. They notice our chosen posture and stance. The positions we take at the table. Our silent presence behind, beside, or out front. The meaning of an extended hand—open, raised, or clenched. How we apply the strength and softness of our touches. Our expressive body language—the flash of a grin, the tilt of a head, the wink of an eye. The depth of our gazes or intensity of our stares.

POWER FUELS OUR SEXUAL FLAME

Sex is one place where you'll encounter the true nature of power in any being.

Powerful people understand the purpose of sexuality: it is our most sacred and profound articulation of intimacy. We offer it selectively through healthy choices. We don't plead, coerce, or bargain with it. We don't overindulge. We create and protect safe spaces, psychologically and physically.

We own our sexuality, in all its forms and manifestations. We know the source: our biological truths, our carnal desires, and our old wounds from which it was forged. We understand the pain of sexual trauma and the many distortions of healthy sexuality propagated around the world.

Most importantly, we control our sex.
Sex doesn't control us.

Our range of sexual expression goes way beyond bucking like a wild stallion, although that can be part of it. As if viewing into our very souls, we channel our powers of mind, body, heart, and spirit to be fully present in the moment. We might engage in light play, primal passion, or complete surrender. We honor the fine mélange of giving, sharing, and receiving.

Sex is but one aspect of our powerful creative fire, our ubiquitous life force. We know how to apply it appropriately, beyond the bedroom. More importantly, we know how to conserve it and fuel it. You'll see nonsexual aspects of our creative fire evidenced in our vocational choices, key relationships, and personal hobbies and pursuits.

THE RISKS OF NOT COMPLETING THE POWER ADVENTURE

Without realizing your true vitality...

your life will begin a steady downward trajectory from the place you're in right now.

You'll fail to connect with both the obvious and unseen power sources streaming around you.

You'll experience a life fading fast into obscurity, defined more by the adventures you declined than the ones you took.

WHAT DOES IT LOOK LIKE WHEN YOU ARE NOT LIVING WITH REAL POWER?

In a word: **irrelevant**.

We all know once-powerful people who lost their vitality. They're the ones still spinning tales of the glory days to dwindling audiences. No longer in the game, like bystanders they stand on the sidelines. They peaked then became frozen in the historical reference of who they were. As the years pass by and the world moves on, we watch them drift to the sidelines.

Sadly, they're desperately yearning to recapture their zest for life. But they're unable to draw inspiration from others or rise to broader possibilities in the world around them. Their own power reserves have become so depleted that even when sparks come their way, there's nothing left in their tanks to rekindle the blaze. They withdraw from any sense of risk, or edge, and relegate themselves to playing small. They are mentally, physically, creatively, emotionally, sexually, spiritually…spent.

One sure sign of desperation and decline:
the minute people start trying to use their power over others.

Our admiration for these folks' past accomplishments slowly fades. Our empathy for their current plights shifts to sympathy. All we hear are complaints about how good things used to be. Eventually we pity their blind inability to discover, retool, and grow simply by getting back in the game playing out right in front of them.

If we're honest, our instinct turns to avoiding such powerless people. Spending too much time with their depleted states drains our power too.

Here are the main risks you face by not renewing your power.

Without the Power Adventure, you'll never trust yourself beyond what you've already come to be, know, and do.

Without the ability to trust yourself in uncertainty, having lost your place in the Arc of Adventure, you will relive the same story, revisit the same lessons, and bump against the same obstacles, over and over. While the scenery and players may vary slightly, you'll be caught in an infinite dead-end loop of your own making.

The more you play to the same old script, the wider the gap will become between you and the rest of life as it continues to evolve. That self-assurance you claimed in the Freedom Adventure will grow stale amidst a sea of change around you. The prosperity you were part of creating on the Courage Adventure will never be enough. You'll force an interpretation of the current world through far too narrow a lens, leaving you pinned down, unable to see things any other way.

Soon, others will come to know you for one thing: being out of date, and out of touch.

You'll constantly talk about not trusting others or what others need to do to earn your trust. Time and time again. But this is all just a thinly veiled response to no longer trusting yourself to adventure further in your own life.

Perpetual mistrust will leave you anywhere but in the present moment, distracted into believing that life keeps happening *to you*, *against you*.

This is where that self-doubt you put to rest in the Freedom Adventure will try to sneak back into your psyche. The louder it gets, the more you'll routinely give your power away. Even worse, your lack of power will start to feel normal. It will become part of your brand—how others perceive and experience you.

You'll show up late, rushed, and frenzied. You'll arrive needing to unload all the extraneous details about where you just came from and how hard it was to extricate yourself just to be here now. Before long, you'll vault into all the endless to-do's waiting when you leave. You know, all the same shit, in a different pile.

But you won't really be *present*. Physically, sure; but mentally, emotionally, and spiritually, you'll be completely absent.

You'll bemoan those who have it easier and drone on about wishing for more time. Meanwhile, you'll fail to find any joy or real meaning with the amount of time you do have (which is suspiciously similar to the available amount of time everyone else has).

Without realizing it, you'll be training your muscle memory to flip-flop between two states: recycled regret about the past and frustrated anxiety about the future.

You're actually training your brain to crave distraction—creating a gushing power leak.

That frantic flipping between past and future comes with another calamity: fooling yourself into believing that constant multitasking is a desirable and sustainable strength.

In fact, this pattern of behavior results in exactly the opposite: an exhausted and weakened brain that knows only noise and interference. You'll find yourself yanked around like a puppet by the very same to-do lists, technology apps and alerts, and calendar tools you put in place to exert more control over your time.

Distraction will become your routine. Any form of mindful rest, mental recovery, or intellectual space for deeper thinking will remain a pipe dream. Sure, you'll keep downloading new time management techniques and meditation apps. But having more to juggle and track will only speed your power drain.

Others will notice how often you rehash the same stories and grievances. Your thinking will become circular, stunting absorption and retention of any new and valuable inputs. In day-to-day interactions, you'll be forever missing the big picture and the hidden gems.

You'll begrudge your lack of downtime, weekend breaks, or real holidays.

Diminishing the value of free time leaves you continuing to work at some ridiculous standard, detracting from your most powerful state: operating with effortless mind, body, heart, and spirit presence with whatever slice of life is right in front of you. In truth, you wouldn't know what to do with free time if someone gifted it to you on a silver platter.

When presented with an open evening, change of scenery, or unforeseen break in the calendar, you revert back to the same old compulsions—pack in more work, revert to impulsive eating or drinking, binge screen time, over process tired topics—leaving you (and those in your company) feeling hollowed out.

This pattern will become so ingrained that you'll stop booking time for yourself, with a romantic partner, or with close friends. You won't be able to fathom how committing to regular, unstructured time would *increase* your power. Taking time to walk on grass, play an instrument, visit a gallery, listen to a podcast on a new topic, or read a fiction novel will seem a waste of time. The prospect of a career sabbatical will seem like something only for the idle rich or something better postponed until retirement.

> **GUIDE TIP:** This might be a good time to pause and ask, "So, what exactly do I do for fun?" What comes up on your list? And then ask, "When was the last time I invested real time in that?" What exactly is getting in your way? Anything besides yourself?

Your limited version of the truth will reign supreme, emotively blocked from seeing things any other way.

An overloaded, overtired mind is no longer able to take stock of a situation from an alternative vantage point.

Starving your magnificent mind of recovery time will leave you overly relying on a small set of pertinent facts, with only your interpretation of their meaning. Your attitude will display shock, even anger, as others offer additional facts and alternative perceptions to the consideration set. You'll become so fixated on changing their facts, you'll be blind to altering your own perceptions.

> *Without harnessing the power to change your own mind, you won't be able to change anything.*

First, your self-awareness will suffer. The same thoughts will trigger the same rote actions and reactions. You'll skip over the emotional current and dull your ability to *feel*. Left in a numb state, you'll experience no *movement*.

Then, you'll lose your ability to self-regulate. You'll blast through each day and completely miss the meaning. You'll complain about feeling hijacked or blindsided, while others describe you as impulsive, quick to blow a fuse, and completely shut down.

You'll fail to recognize yourself as an active variable in the mix, either as part of the solution or part of the problem. That amount of cognitive dissonance is off-putting. Over time, others will tune you out and eventually move on—sadly, especially those you most want and need in your corner.

You'll tout a false, self-fulfilling mantra: "I'm just not good with change." And things will spiral downward from there.

At some point, those who admire your critical-thinking strengths also will want to tap into your creative-thinking capacity and engage in the light, intuitive, and daring parts of your mental makeup. Gripped by the need to see things only your way, you'll remain blocked from the full capacity of your magnificent mind. You'll be rendered ill-equipped to transform with change and unable to choose to move beyond the quick fix on any adventure.

> *Denying your own creativity will have*
> *you denying creativity in the world around you.*
> *And it will show.*

You'll never crack the code to reveal that next inspiring realization of your career, leisure time, or romantic life. Art, fashion, and design will seem frivolous and impractical. You'll stick with the same foods and restaurants.

Natural beauties will go unnoticed. Sexual experiences will become awkward, transactional, or downright boring. When arriving in a new place, introduced to a new person, or invited on a first-time adventure, you'll show up pre-wired for a negative appraisal:

- *The water here isn't as good. This room is subpar. That sounds too far.*

- *I thought she'd be taller. I assumed they'd be more inspiring. He wasn't that smart.*

- *This trek is nothing like Nepal. I thought the Mona Lisa would be bigger. If you've seen one old monument, you've seen them all.*

In the face of a novel idea, a challenge to the status quo, plaid mixed with stripes, playful teasing, or a new flavor profile, your reactions will suck the joy out of the moment:

"Oh, that's _____." *Stupid. Silly. Ludicrous. Dumb. Gross. Useless.*

Such responses are telltale signs of low-power reserves. They work only to speed your downward slide, shutting down all access to adventure.

Running with your power tank on empty guarantees a sluggish, rapidly aging physical body.

You don't stop being active because your body is declining. Your body is declining because you've stopped being active.

Evidence of nagging, untreated ailments and injuries are easy to overlook. But steady neglect will eventually land you in one of those massively disruptive reckonings. High-performance race cars take regular pit stops for a reason.

One day you'll notice your pulse quicken going up a flight of stairs. Your gait will feel off. You'll find that your weakened core has collapsed your natural height. Countless hours of stationary screen time have compressed your upper spine, shut off blood flow, caused pinched nerves, and strained your eyes, head, neck, and shoulders. Your skin has become pasty, and your hair and nails look malnourished. Your gut is bloated. Your sleep is irregular. You can no longer touch your toes. You eat standing up, during meetings, or on the move. Your energy comes and goes. Your mood is erratic.

No, it's not all genetics or the fallout from one crazy night out. You've been driving your body hard while neglecting the engine lights and warning gauges. You keep waiving off the pit stops and maintenance crews for some more immediate impulse. You rely on your own shoddy workarounds to get you through one more lap.

Sure, your body *will* work from behind a desk, when glued to a screen, or after hours on the couch, but that's hardly what it was designed for.

And really, are any of those places conducive for finding adventure?

How much longer are you going to treat this one-of-a-kind, phenomenal physical machine you've been gifted like some tired old meat sack to use and abuse? When one day it gives out, don't say you weren't warned.

With *all* that going on, it's no wonder when your sex life has become so _____.

Only you can fill in the blank because only you know the real truth:

Starved. Shameful. Void. Frustrated. Blocked. Compulsive. Repetitive. Boring. Tedious. Unfulfilling. Purposeless.

Whatever it is, you're living it.

Failing to step into your true power—that harmonious interplay between mind, body, heart, and spirit—leaves you sensually underdeveloped. Sexually immature.

If your sex holds claim over you versus you claiming it, I feel for you. Unresolved traumas and compulsive afflictions manifest into secret lives of deep and hidden pain. Impulsive urges get treated like mosquito bites—hurriedly scratched for temporary relief, while the overall irritation increases. Meanwhile, your real power and primal potency remains buried or hidden in shame.

If your sex life is wrapped in constant bartering, pleading, pouting, stalling, or otherwise manipulating to get your way, you're giving away the very essence of your power. You'll give when you really want to receive, and receive when you really want to give. You'll trudge along unfulfilled and unaware of the spectacular spectrum of intimate experiences and mature lovemaking.

To your partner, you'll come across as needy, childish, juvenile, unapproachable, and decidedly unsexy. Incapable of creating or holding a safe and loving space for your own sexuality, you'll have no context from which to appreciate and create such a space with another. Never revealing unspoken yearnings leaves your partner guessing and each of you frustrated. Desperation may lead you to believe the only way to become truly satisfied is to use your still immature sexuality as power *over* others.

For many, the failure to mature sexually is perhaps the ultimate power drain, an incalculably limiting factor to a life fully lived. We all know how misguided sexuality is capable of inflicting grave wounds. We're all too familiar with the stories of devastated marriages and personal lives, toppled political careers, ruined professional reputations, and prison sentences. Tragically, such negative shock waves envelope those in the immediate blast radius and resonate further harm far beyond the initial lapse or transgression.

To be absolutely clear, renewing your sexual power is NOT about increasing frequency or demanding any particular sex act. It's about opening up to *all* of your essential power sources, *combined*—your magnificent mind, capable body, generous heart, and irrepressible spirit. It's about unleashing the cumulative total of your entire life force, breaking from the shell of what used to be.

> **GUIDE TIP:** Whew, that's a lot to take in. Recall what we said at the outset. If you find yourself relating to any of this, you have the power to do something about it. But nothing will change if you don't acknowledge the truth of your current reality and start owning your own next steps on the Power Adventure.

SO, WHAT LIES AHEAD ON THE POWER ADVENTURE?

The Courage Adventure was all about creating collective prosperity and thriving in relationships of interdependence. And you did. But shifting into autopilot now will leave you ill-prepared for what lies ahead. Now is the time to revitalize your primal potency, expand beyond your prior limits, and cherish each moment you're alive.

The Power Adventure is about embodying a vital life by employing all the essential elements of your divine design. It's about living full, here and now, regardless of situation or circumstance. It's about respecting the impermanence in all things and rising to the sanctity of your time left on earth. It requires you to grow beyond familiar comforts and their inherent limits.

It's also about preparing you for the mystery of what lies ahead—the big transitions, including death and whatever comes after. No matter how much you think you have it all figured out, of one thing you may be sure: life isn't done with you yet. More disruption, natural endings, and new beginnings await. The Power Adventure is what keeps your flame burning hot, agile, effortless, and, at all times, adventure-ready.

Unlike the Freedom and Courage Adventures, which involved three stages to complete, the Power Adventure is done in four stages, one for each of the four essential elements of your divine design. In these stages, you learn how to rejuvenate your:

- Vision—the natural power in your irrepressible spirit.
- Empathy—the natural power in your generous heart.
- Presence—the natural power in your magnificent mind.
- Bravery—the natural power in your physical body.

Here are the headlines of what you most need to know.

The Power Adventure invites evolution and requires your commitment to never being "done."

Yes, the Courage Adventure is an incredible rewarding experience. It's also packed full of endless planning and juggling. Your life gets so cluttered it can't help but also become overly complicated. No matter how large and in-charge your successes have left you feeling, you're wise enough to know that constant change, in all forms, is just part of the deal.

Or did your ego fool you into believing your success was somehow beyond the impermanence of all things?

The Power Adventure is where you discard that which no longer serves you in order to make space for new discoveries. It's about *cultivating* a life in progress, continual *individuation*, lest all that accumulation and complacency dulls your edge or douses your flame. That's what makes the Power Adventure so daunting. Because it dares you to rise above your past successes and failures, to trade them all for power in the here-and-now, to grow *with* and *through* the fire of what is most challenging, real, and relevant.

Here are some of the tests you can expect along the Power Adventure.

Your professional identity will get tested. Who you are beyond the career you've built, away from colleagues, and outside of patterned work routines.

Your definition of work and workplace will be tested. Intertwined with the meaning you ascribe to home and happiness, money and wealth. What does the word "legacy" conjure for you? Expect the "scarcity versus abundance" question to keep calling until you answer.

Your lover, children, and family will test you. Each wants to stay connected with the *real* you, the one behind all the accomplishment and accumulation. They want to be seen and celebrated, in the richness of their own adventures with freedom, courage, and power, and not cast in the mold of who you still want them to be.

How you relate to sex and intimacy will get tested. A whole new world of deeper, more meaningful physical sensation and spiritual arousal is within your reach, if you have the power to invite it in. You can have the capacity to give and receive, with assertive ease. To gift yourself or another a timeless float in blissful surrender.

Your body and mind will test you. As the natural aging process settles in, your resilience and resourcefulness will test you to discover new sources of vitality and acuity. Your ability to boldly step into the unknown will be tested and, right along with it, your sense of care and compassion, for yourself most of all.

And let's not forget how your soul will be tested. You'll be facing legacy and mortality, mired in existential questions and imperfect answers, in search of the meaning of it all.

> **GUIDE TIP:** Remember, disruptions are constant, and that's not a bad thing. With or without your permission, they exist to keep you at your best, present with all that is real, here and now. Just when you've built an operating system to handle it all, the next program glitch will arrive right on cue, testing your mettle once again. This is a good time to take note of which of these tests are already visiting you—or about to come calling for your attention.

The Power Adventure is about respecting the impermanence in all things and never taking the sanctity of life for granted.

The Power Adventure holds moments of awe, mystery, and grace, patiently waiting to be unveiled in the omnipresent cycle of birth, life, death, and rebirth. It draws your attention to the fluid nature of time, past, present, and future. It holds the wisdom that all things must pass and reminds us there is no dress rehearsal. How we choose to *be* in the potential of this day, this hour, this minute is all we really have.

> **GUIDE TIP:** Look at the calendar. What day is it? Try saying this aloud, filling in your own blanks:
>
> "Today is [month], [day], [year].
> This day is still happening,

> and once over, will never happen again.
> What will I make of the time I have left?"
>
> And as you begin to comprehend what that means for you, another moment you'll never have again just slipped by. In the Power Adventure, the only time is *now*.

The Power Adventure sparks a redefinition of relative "worth."

All of these tests have a common purpose: to keep your fire hot enough to burn away the excess, to reveal only that which is *most* worth taking forward—the basic ingredients of life to hold tightly to and build from.

That necessitates a shift in how you assess the price of realizing the life you most want to inhabit. Often that starts by decreasing the value placed on *tangible* assets (money, home, houses, car or cars, stuff, and material possessions) and increasing the value placed on *intangible* assets (quality moments, genuine connections, health and wellness, the feeling of vitality at the beginning and ending of each day, lived experience, autonomy, peace of mind).

> *This is your moment to take inventory, declutter, and simplify your life around the precious few priorities that matter most.*

It's time to elevate your altitude—by dumping excess cargo, soaring to new heights, and being present with the realities that now require your full attention.

It's time to expand your attitude—by leading yourself forward with self-compassion and maturing your grit and resolve to see new disruptions not as annoyance, but as the next challenge designed to keep your adventure game honest and potent.

> **GUIDE TIP:** Don't expect to make it through unscathed. But keep your eyes on the prize, heart open, head clear, and body active, and, not only will you make it through in one piece, you'll emerge stronger from all those bumps, bruises, and blisters. Each step on the Power Adventure leaves you feeling born again. You'll sleep well, knowing that if this day is to be your last, your flame burned bright until the end.

The Power Adventure opens the door to your own undiscovered country.

It's the place to tap the innermost aspects of your being and brings into focus that version of yourself you have yet to become. It invites you to the edge—*your* edge. It has an ingenious way of drawing from each of your essential elements, asking questions that call upon your deepest power sources:

- What next, greatest adventure is beckoning me forward? (Unleash your irrepressible spirit to vision positive possibilities in your life ahead.)

- Why is that so important to me, now? (Arouse your generous heart to be empathetic to your deepest motivations and desires.)

- To realize that, what realities are most deserving of my complete attention? (Stimulate your magnificent mind to be present with the facts staring you in the face.)

- With that clarity, what am I willing to leave behind and what bold, energizing move am I willing to step into? (Activate your bravery in the physical world.)

The Power Adventure keeps you honest with *all* aspects of your divine design.

> **GUIDE TIP:** It all starts by defining a powerful vision for your future. One that captures the dreams and desires of your irrepressible spirit. Without that, you'll juggle too many ideas and spin your wheels in self-doubt. If, in the end, you're not willing to let go of what's holding you back (you know, the real price of realizing the life you were designed for), your emotional, intellectual, and physical moves will be tentative and uninspiring. No one will take you seriously, and your momentum will never get off the ground.

In the end, the Power Adventure embodies your time on earth and how you will be remembered.

Early steps in the Power Adventure may feel like going back to preschool. Resisting that will make it harder to establish sufficient traction. Instead, liberate that childlike openness and you'll hit the ground running. Either way, expect to get your hands messy again, digging in the dirt of self-discovery and self-disclosure. Stepping into shadows, befriending darkness, and exploring the edges of what you find.

Consider your essential vision, empathy, presence, and bravery. You claimed them in the Freedom Adventure. You put them to purposeful use in the Courage Adventure. Now it's time to revitalize, rejuvenate, and interconnect these aspects of your primal potency as you never have before.

You'll find yourself stepping to the brink, boldly going where you haven't gone before. Peeling back the layers. Shedding old fears. Breathing new oxygen into the most vital aspects of your nature. Facing the deepest aspects of who you are and making peace with who you find. Opening doors that lead toward all you are now ready to become. Harnessing every ounce of growth to prepare you for whatever comes next.

It's about challenging yourself to personify all you discover, leaving you equipped for any adventure to come.

In the end, that's what makes the Power Adventure the most effortless. Because you're left operating at a level *above* it all. Ready, willing, and able to push all your chips into the pot. To go all-in with the vast and vivacious. The simple and sublime. The radical and radiant. The puissant and pulsating. The timeless and transcendent.

And then, do it all again. Forever at home in the unknown and unknowable.

The pages ahead highlight the heart-racing, mind-blowing, life-altering thrills awaiting you and the risks of letting your power sources flame out or run dry.

> **GUIDE TIP:** This adventure can be wildly fun, but it is **not** about reckless thrill seeking. It's about a supreme respect for life itself, holding sacred the precious potential in each moment and letting nothing else get in your way.

THE POWER ADVENTURE TRAIL GUIDE: WHAT WILL BE HARD AT FIRST AND HOW TO KEEP ADVANCING FORWARD

Nothing is hard this time about the Arc of Adventure. From that initial disruptive spark to the prize that awaits, you know what to expect.

This time, however, the strange and inexplicable nature of Power Adventure disruptions are meant for you alone. They show up in ways you can't quite fathom until they happen. Simple and obvious. Complex and mind-boggling. All at once. They leave you shaking your head, maybe smiling in awe. You'll be tempted to keep them to yourself, lest others think you've lost your marbles. Except there are others who have been there too, and they will share and celebrate your wonder, reverence, and delight.

> **GUIDE TIP:** Freedom adventure disruptions are largely internal, and Courage Adventure disruptions mainly external. Your experiences on the Power Adventure will be different, best described as otherworldly. This time, get ready for disruptions to be delivered by forces far beyond your control or comprehension.

Here are a few of the impediments to expect, along with the usual guide tips on how to enjoy your progress.

You're not in Kansas anymore.

Get ready to pull back the curtain and enter a whole new world of technicolor.

The Power Adventure is as multidimensional as you want to make it. The interconnected bonds between the elements of your divine design and their respective power sources are universal. Ethereal. Bigger and beyond any one of us. We can never truly *know* them. It's enough to be with them at the point of convergence where they swirl around us, surge through us, and drift beyond us.

You'll be invited to interact with elements of earth (your source of presence), water (your source of empathy), fire (your source of bravery), and sky (your source of vision) in new ways that are intermingled and integrated.

On your Power Adventure, anything goes:

- Probe the hermetic laws of mentalism, correspondence, vibration, polarity, rhythm, cause and effect, and the duality of gender.

- Explore your natural hindrances and the noblest of truths.

- Understand the universal suffering of pain, change, and conditionality.

- Challenge and expand your physical presence, sensory sensitivity, and sexual acuity.

- Deepen your wisdom, stimulate your mental capacity, and build new neural pathways through the joy of *not* knowing.

- Confidently surf with your unprotected heart on waves of joy, breakers of grief, and everything between.

- Open new doors to spirit worlds that float beyond the confines of an ego-driven mind.

- ...and so much more.

GUIDE TIP: If this feels a little crazy, or at least counterintuitive, that's normal. It may be a daunting proposition to release your past correlations—correlating power with force, effort with struggle, and goals with achievement. But you're ready to operate at a higher altitude and expanded attitude, which is exactly what's required to maximize the Power Adventure.

Initially, your sense of power will be oriented to retaining control. That's the first thing to shift (and the sooner, the better).

The more you achieved in the Courage Adventure, the more tempting it may be to believe that your singular job is to maintain power *over* your environment, so as to protect yourself, your loved ones, and everything you've built. To keep things comfortable, just as they are. And if you still believe power is scarce, your every move will be geared toward grabbing it, conserving it, and hoarding it.

Since true power is limitless, that's the kind of wheel spinning to shift out of. ASAP.

Remember, we're on our way to a whole new altitude and attitude in how we think about power. You're here to unlock the door to a higher order of what power might mean for you: mind, body, heart, and spirit. Your very own sustainable power ecosystem.

Challenging? Sure. Demanding? Yes.

Yet ultimately effortless in the execution. That's the prize worth working toward.

This adventure requires you to trust in what lies ahead more than in what you're leaving behind.

Yes, you can trust that all the ways you understood and utilized your power up to this point were not *wrong*. In fact, all prior experiences with power were supremely valuable and *necessary* to get you to this point.

But now, those former power orientations are no longer contextually appropriate. They've become insufficient and inefficient. Relying on them any further, to any degree, will only slow you down or leave you stuck.

Feeling strong tugs back to "what was" is normal. That's grief doing its work to help ensure you say a proper goodbye. Be assured, the essential lessons of the past are still with you, and any resource you need will avail itself to you.

Be sure to take ample time for this step. To trust in new sources of power, you've got to clear your mind, body, heart, and spirit, just as you would firmly close one door and swing open another. You want to come to complete closure with those old power orientations, forever.

> **GUIDE TIP:** Before you can shift your trust to what lies ahead, you've got to dispose of the ways you used to trust your power. Kind of like taking out the trash. Or hosting a retirement party in which you acknowledge and thank your old ways for years of dedicated, faithful service. Hang a photo as a sober reminder to never go back or present a gift that marks a fond farewell to all you've left behind.

The ride into new power orientations will feel like a roller coaster. Expect to oscillate between exhilaration and despair.

As the terrain becomes less comfortable, familiar, and predictable, you'll question yourself.

Instead: trust yourself in the wild unknown.

This is the land of discovery. You're going to experience natural endings and new beginnings. You'll ride euphoric highs and confront sorrowful lows before, once again, finding yourself back on the rise.

The trick is to suspend any expectation of what you *think* you'll find, or even *want* or *hope* to find. Choose instead to stay open and keenly alert to whatever comes your way.

Your sense of power is being rebuilt from sources you have yet to fully grasp. It's likely you won't end up with the exact Power Adventure you *want*, but stay with it, and you're guaranteed to come away with the exact power experience you *need*.

*The more you travel forward,
the more that place you came from will
become a distant and fond memory.*

> **GUIDE TIP:** It's only from the place you're currently standing that the future looks so daunting. Keep your mind, body, heart, and spirit all moving steadily forward. Some days, you'll make huge strides. Savor those and know you're banking reserves for tougher days ahead. When those days arrive, you'll do well just to hold your ground. Lean into the wind, knowing it will soon be at your back again.

Expect to assume your Power Adventure is done before it actually is.

In the early stages of feeling your power renew, you'll be tempted to start reasserting control. You'll want to start naming things, attaching meaning, and concluding that now you "know."

Another part of you may feel guilty that you're investing so much in yourself. You may start to think it is time to return to normal and get back to your busy life. You might even question whether any of this is worthwhile.

Instead, trust that your power is still cultivating. Trust there is more to explore, deeper discovery and guidance to be had. Remember, this type of power is borne of abundance. It's limitless. Accordingly, you have no real way to gauge how powerful you might actually become.

As you move further and further into uncharted space, keep breathing, observing, and assimilating. Let things percolate. Stay on the path of what feels pure, clean, real, and blissful.

> *Like a painter, you know*
> *the importance of those final brush strokes*
> *and will recognize the moment when*
> *your canvas is complete.*

GUIDE TIP: Just as you begin to feel more powerful, relative to historical standards, you're at risk of imposing make-believe limits on your power potential. Disembark from the Power Adventure too early, and you'll sabotage all prior investments and find yourself right back in the life you left behind. Another false start. Trust me, you'll know when you've arrived at that place of truly effortless power. And you'll know exactly what to do next.

Fellow adventurer, this is a very good time for an impromptu pause.

We're about to take our last, long, and honest look in the mirror. After riding high in the Courage Adventure, this level of raw introspection can feel daunting, disheartening, even frightening. You're bound to recognize some part of yourself you'd prefer to keep hidden from others, or from yourself.

Confronting whatever uncomfortable or inconvenient truth that comes up for you is what I refer to as "stepping into the fire" (recall the full meaning of that essential element of your design). Our intention in approaching what may look too hot to handle (at least on the surface) or poking at some old scab (that you've become accustomed to suffering through) is not to make you feel even worse. The intent is not for you to shrink back, so demoralized that you decide to quit before even starting.

Instead, the point is to engage the fire in you to burn through the bullshit and blaze a trail toward a whole new level of trust:

- Trust in all you know about yourself and what you took away from the Freedom Adventure: that you belong in this moment, and it to you.

- Trust in all you learned by showing yourself to the world during the Courage Adventure: that you can create and thrive in relationships of prosperous interdependence.

- Now it's time to trust that you're not done growing. Trust that there is more vitality in you, and beyond you, that is meant for you to discover. Trust that every past step has prepared you to overcome any threat, obstacle, or challenge and make it to the blissfully calm, wonderfully warm waters awaiting you on the other side.

Remember, this is more than just the next adventure in a three-ring adventure circus. The Power Adventure is the most *daunting*, most *daring*. The truth is, I know there are untapped power sources in you…even if you don't quite believe it yet. Stick with it, and you too will unearth rewards beyond any fear or risk you'll face along the way. That's why in the end, you'll also come to know the Power Adventure as the most *exhilarating*.

Ready, steady, let's go.

• • •

WARM-UP

First you learned how to breathe freedom. Then you practiced breathing courage by slowing down, taking even breaths, extending each breathing step, and paying attention to the space between breaths.

The final warm-up blends breathing and meditation. With practice, you'll be able to effortlessly summon the sort of power you want most—mental, emotional, physical, spiritual—from your very own reservoir of vitality anytime, anywhere.

> **GUIDE TIP:** News flash for those who claim not to meditate or not to know how: you're meditating constantly, by virtue of the thoughts you consciously load or subconsciously allow to loiter and captivate your mind. For better or worse.
>
> Simply, meditation is the practice of intentionally focusing one's mind for a period of time. You're going to intentionally direct your mind to a particular power source, for a particular period of time... both of which you will decide.
>
> If you are ready to go beyond the simple version we'll try here, look up some of the more in-depth techniques and see what grabs your interest. Shamanic, Taoist, or Tiger breathing (to name a few). Metta (loving-kindness), guided, Vipassana, or Transcendental Meditation (to name a few). Thai massage, Reiki, reflexology, and working with chakras. Maybe somewhere in there lies your next Power Adventure.

Breathing your power.

You've learned how each component of our human divine design has an elemental representation (vision = air, presence = earth, empathy = water, bravery = fire). You've learned that in isolation, each signifies essential counter-balancing aspects of the divine feminine and the divine masculine, and when applied together, they unlock the Axes of Adventure. You've also learned the importance of individually applying these components in their purest forms versus diluting their true power by blending them together in a single application.

Setting aside ancient meaning and metaphor, it's important to appreciate how these power elements manifest, or are embodied in the practical, day-to-day, real world. No doubt you have encountered countless coaches, therapists, books, videos, and apps encouraging you to be more mindful (aka to be more present). The wide variety of mindfulness exercises that follow have one thing in common: breathing.

On your Power Adventures, you'll want to be more than just "mind full." The winning move is to deepen your connection with the embodiment of each element in order to summon the power needed most, in any given situation, and apply its purest form with ease. So in the same vein, we will learn how to direct our breath to be:

Spirit-centered—harnesses the air element, leveling up more vision in order to dream up inspiring ideas and positive possibilities.

Mind-centered—harnesses the earth element, leveling up more presence in order to focus the mind on achieving deeper wisdoms and truths.

Heart-centered—harnesses the water element, leveling up more empathy in order to harness emotions that heal and create compassionate connections.

Body-centered—harnesses the fire element, leveling up more bravery in order to act with assertive autonomy in the face of fear and risk.

The key to it all is somatic breathing, or the intentional directing of breath into specific areas of the body so you sense how each power source resides in your physical form. With practice, you'll be able to interpret the sensations that ensure your vitality is topped-up and flowing with steady ease. You'll be able to summon the power you want most, in any given situation, anytime, anywhere.

And yes, let's steer clear of getting too literal. We can agree that by any technical, biological, or scientific definition, emotions don't reside in the four chambers of your heart, and gut instincts don't reside in the layered folds of your small and large intestines. We're just tapping into widely understood and therefore useful associations.

Final reminder. While each of the Freedom and Courage Adventures had three expedition stages to complete, the Power Adventure has four: one for each of the essential power sources.

Let's do it.

Find your comfortable seated, standing, or lying-down position. Repattern that fluid, evenly paced, four-step breathing rhythm. Soften your eyes. Relax the muscles in your forehead and face.

When you feel ready, pick one of your elemental power sources to tap into. Continue your even, slow, intentional breathing and follow these simple prompts.

To tap into the power of your irrepressible spirit:

- Tilt your gaze skyward. Raise arms up and out, in full victory pose. Smile in silent triumph. Tune in to your limitless spiritual energy and imagine past, present, and future intertwined in a blissful single moment of belonging. You are floating in a universe of infinite possibility.

- *Once in that zone you may want to ask: what positive future inspires me to go beyond anything I have yet to experience?*

- Keep breathing as you patiently await a powerful image to materialize.

To tap into the power of your magnificent mind:

- Gently place your hands on your head. Tune in to your mental circuit board, the complex exchange of thoughts, images, and voices steadily moving and interacting. Pick one to focus on, see it in isolation, and set it adrift in exchange for the next one. If any fight to recapture your focus, note that too, and again set them adrift. Keep going until your mind feels less cluttered and clearer.

- *Once in that zone, you may want to ask: what is most real, most true, most irrefutable around me now?*

- Keep breathing as you patiently await a powerful wisdom to be revealed.

To tap into the power of your holistic heart:

- Bring both hands over your heart. Tune in to the steady life pulse, like a calm tide, drifting in, drifting out. With each new wave, feel yourself becoming less guarded, less blocked. Feel the rough edges being smoothed away, revealing unresolved grief, trauma, or pain. Healing through lightness, laughter, and love.

- *Once in that zone, you may want to ask: what emotions are most alive in me?*

- Keep breathing as you patiently await a powerful understanding to rise up.

Tap into the power of your capable body:

- Lower both hands to your belly. Tune into the truth held in your gut. That sensory buzz of all systems go. That feeling when your beautiful physical machine is in full motion, each step forward lit by the torch of your primal fire. That intuitive knowing to strike while the iron is hot, moving boldly forward into the unknown.

- *Once in this zone, you may want to ask: what next move is my moment to seize?*

- Keep breathing as you patiently await the call to a powerful action.

Keep in mind that any sort of meditation practice is just that: a practice you'll need to revisit regularly. You can't do one session and expect everything to fall into place.

At first it may feel impossible to slow down your mind. You may feel frustrated that "nothing is happening." Don't judge. Just observe, keep breathing, and try again tomorrow. The simple act of taking the time and space for yourself will pay dividends from day one.

Start with five or ten minutes each day for a week. Then a second week. If you stay with it, I guarantee your power will start to shift. And the beauty is we don't need to understand what's happening or why it's working. Just trust that innate power sources are rising inside you—inside your spirit, mind, heart, and gut—all coming online as you continue your adventure practice.

* * *

STAGE 1:
Unleash Your Irrepressible Spirit

*This first expedition on the
Power Adventure is all about looking up to
dream and imagine inspiring possibilities
"outside the box" of any reality
you've experienced so far.*

Follow the flow of activities below, or use them to inspire a version of your own. Use your newfound breathing/meditation technique to revitalize your vision and grow the power of your irrepressible spirit. Draw also from your presence, empathy, and bravery as you follow the Arc of Adventure that unfolds.

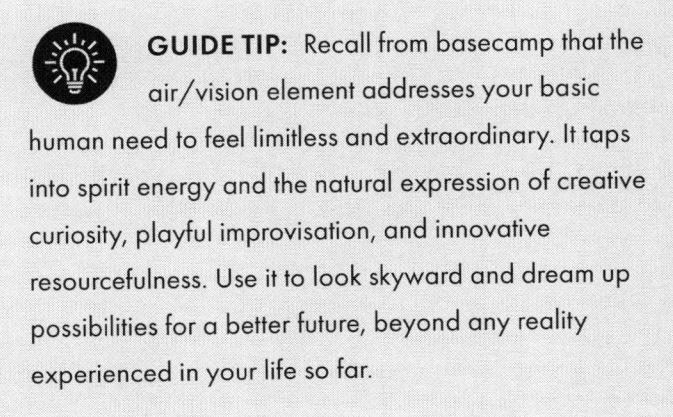

> **GUIDE TIP:** Recall from basecamp that the air/vision element addresses your basic human need to feel limitless and extraordinary. It taps into spirit energy and the natural expression of creative curiosity, playful improvisation, and innovative resourcefulness. Use it to look skyward and dream up possibilities for a better future, beyond any reality experienced in your life so far.

> Remember the source of your true vision is internal and soul driven. It exists without concern for external validation, constraints, or the "how" for any ideas to come to fruition.

Explore the deeper meaning of the air/vision power element.

- Trace the etymology of words like spirit, soul, and vision. What resonates beyond your initial definitions? What other words compel you to discover more? What common concepts keep showing up?

- Where might you find metaphorical, symbolic, or mythical representation across time periods, cultures, and art forms? If you had to design your own symbol for this power element, what would it entail? A light bulb? A thunderbolt? A starry sky?

- Research the practices used around the world to generate greater vision and rejuvenate spiritual power, such as:

Solo or guided quests related to coming of age, rebirth, or renewed purpose.

Use of natural substances to invite visionary breakthroughs.

Connection to animal energies, astrological signs, or other cosmic forces.

- Start drafting your list of possible spirit adventures. Which ones are calling to the dreamer in you?

Conduct an audit: where in your life is vision over- or under-represented?

- Test this by asking, "What inspiring idea or positive possibility is calling to me?"

- Assemble blank paper and colored pencils, pens, or markers. Draw a picture that captures your biggest aspirations and most glorious, uninhibited desires for your dream future.

- Note how much fun you have freeform drawing and how easy it is to access your creative juices:

Are you playful and effortless in your use of color, white space, dimension, and detail?

Are you flustered or blocked in a mindset of "I can't draw," "What's the point?" or "This is stupid?" Still staring at the blank page?

Use open-ended questions to light up your next big idea.

- Sift through everything pulling at your attention to reveal a single far-reaching, slightly daunting, existential theme or open-ended question you want to explore.

- Whether your question begins with "why, what, how, when, where, or who," make it personal to you, timely, important, and concise. Possibilities include:

    What is the meaning of _____ *for me now?* (money, sex, work, parenting, home, travel, marriage…)

    How would I show up in this _____ *if it were to be my last?* (day, week, month, year, decade…or job, project, trip, relationship…)

    What am I gripping too tightly? What am I holding too loosely? What do I most not *want to talk about?* (my identity with status, wealth, health, my body, mortality, legacy…)

    What is my next greatest adventure? (Answer determined by keeping all the noise and distractions at bay and letting the silence do the work…)

It's go time! Your spirit adventures await!

- Which of your discoveries feel intriguing, worth pursuing, and most calling to the adventurer in you? Does how you feel now resonate with any other times from your past?

- What symbol, totem, or type of energy best represents your irrepressible spirit then and now? How will you draw from that to fuel more spiritual growth in your life today?

- Is there a quote, photo, book, movie, piece of art, or song that you want to rally around? Pick the ones you connect with most and explore ways to keep them front and center in your day-to-day world. Curate your own personal "spirit quote list" or song playlist.

- Which real or fictional characters have storylines that embody the power of spirit in a way you find personally meaningful? Name the top three attributes you want to personify in your own life.

- Do more research analysis, as if you were the studio director in charge of central casting. For those characters you've identified: what factors determine how they spend their time? What passions are they devoted to? What hobbies peak their interests? How do they dress and conduct themselves?

Who do they affiliate with and who do they steer clear of? What is the creed by which they live?

- What parts of those character profiles will you borrow from and turn into your own?

- What single big idea might be your next wake-up call? Write it down. Speak it aloud clearly and slowly. Imagine it displayed in neon lights on a gigantic billboard that you see from wherever you are. Post it in your workspace, on your bathroom mirror, or on your kitchen refrigerator. Share it openly with those around you.

- What adventure opportunities will you now create to explore your big idea? Perhaps you'll:

  Make time for a dedicated solo trip or pilgrimage.

  Engage a qualified resource to help design a bespoke experience or be in your corner as a trusted guide.

  Sign up for a vision quest workshop or multi-day silent retreat.

  Or…?

Hold space for powerful ideas and spiritual inputs to find their way into your day-to-day routines.

STAGE 2:
Stimulate Your Magnificent Mind

This second expedition is all about evolving your intellect to be sharp and clear with what is most real, most essential, and most worthy of your best and complete attention.

Follow the flow of activities below or use them to inspire a version of your own. Use your newfound breathing/meditation technique to revitalize your presence and grow the power of your magnificent mind. Draw also from your vision, empathy, and bravery as you follow the Arc of Adventure that unfolds.

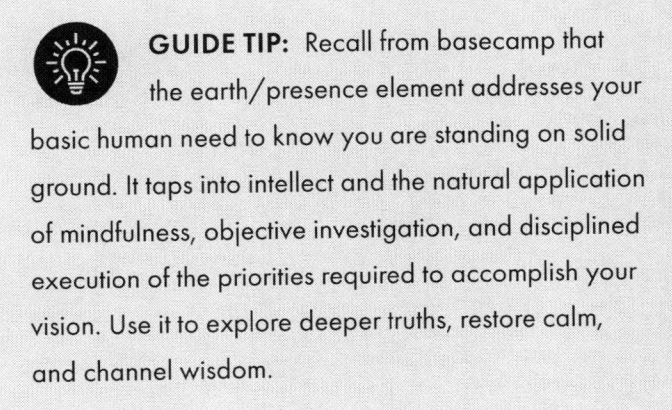

> **GUIDE TIP:** Recall from basecamp that the earth/presence element addresses your basic human need to know you are standing on solid ground. It taps into intellect and the natural application of mindfulness, objective investigation, and disciplined execution of the priorities required to accomplish your vision. Use it to explore deeper truths, restore calm, and channel wisdom.

> Remember, intellect is best sharpened through structured and unstructured methods, while keeping sight of the big picture. Deeper knowledge becomes possible as you embrace **not** knowing and the joy of first-time learning.

Explore the deeper meaning of the earth/presence power element.

- Trace the etymology of words like earth, wisdom, and presence. What resonates beyond your initial definitions? What other words compel you to discover more? What common concepts keep showing up?

- Where might you find metaphorical, symbolic, or mythical representation across time periods, cultures, and art forms? If you had to design your own symbol for this power element what would it entail? A tree in bloom? A magnifying glass? The scales of wisdom and justice?

- Research the practices used around the world to generate greater presence and rejuvenate mental power, such as:

  Memory games and tricks to sharpen concentration and recall.

  Methods to stimulate left- and right-brain acuity.

  Common mindfulness techniques of stoics, monks, and lifelong learners.

  The role of technology, nutrition, natural light, time outdoors, and rest (all of which can work to help or hinder your magnificent mind).

- Start drafting your list of possible mind adventures. Which ones are calling to the learner in you?

Conduct an audit: where in your life is the ability to be present over- or under-represented?

- Test this by asking, "What single fact, decision, or question is most deserving of my complete attention at this time?"

- Make a list of all the thoughts, priorities, and distractions in your head. Or draw a pictorial representation of what's going on inside your brain. Note in your drawing how much of your mental activity is allocated to:

Anticipating the future (for better or worse).

Recycling the past (for better or worse).

- How much capacity is left to be present with what is most real, most calling for your complete focus?

Embrace "not knowing" to separate fact from fiction and discover deeper truths.

- Research the primary learning types. Start with visual, auditory, and kinesthetic learning, and expand your understanding from there.

  Which is your most practiced? Where have you relied on it?

  What is your least practiced? Where might it be useful? What immediate opportunities exist to step into it?

- Stop getting swept away by opinion-based discussions and debates around the water cooler or at the dinner table. Stop feeding, breeding or stoking propaganda, especially of the anonymous, social media variety. Instead:

  When hearing a recount that challenges your view or prior knowledge, don your detective hat and go to the source.

Practice asking objective questions.

Conduct your own primary research to learn actual facts.

Uncover and bring forward expert knowledge, historical lessons, and timeless truths from other disciplines, cultures, genres, and generations.

It's go time! Your mind adventures await!

- Which of your discoveries feel intriguing, worth pursuing, and most calling to the adventurer in you? Does how you feel now resonate with any other times from your past?

- What symbol, totem, or type of energy best represents your magnificent mind then and now? How will you draw from that to fuel more intellectual growth in your life today?

- It's time to build some new neural pathways. Pick a new topic to start learning about, like you were back in grade school—the more obscure, the better. Better yet, roll the dice or let someone pick the topic for you. Perhaps:

    Enroll in a lecture series or course. Read five research papers on the same topic.

Study, dissect, and rebuild a model, object, or piece of machinery.

Listen to experts debate both sides of a topic. Distill arguments on both sides for yourself.

Sign up for an all-in, hands-on, experiential learning workshop.

Create a virtual classroom outdoors—anywhere but behind your desk.

- Invest in dedicated structured and nonstructured learning times, for example:

  Learn another language through an app. For full cultural immersion dedicate a conversation or entire day to communicating only in that new language.

  Invest time in solitary silence. Step into a new form of meditation by following a particular practice or asking an expert guide to lead you. Start with a few minutes upon waking, during an afternoon walk, or before bed.

  Experiment with how your mind performs in both highly stimulating and purely void environments. Try listening to an audio lecture while in a sensory deprivation tank.

  Work out your mental muscles through puzzles and games, arithmetic and calculations, expanded vocabulary, interpretive art, and creative play and competition.

- Track your notes and share your observations with others who share your commitment to stimulating, ongoing intellectual expansion.

Dedicate real space in your life to follow the learning trails that unfold in front of you.

> **STAGE 3:**
>
> **Expand Your Holistic Heart**

This third expedition is all about fueling the flow of kind and compassionate connections within yourself, with others, and the world around you.

Follow the flow of activities below or use them to inspire a version of your own. Use your newfound breathing/meditation technique to revitalize your empathy and grow the power of your holistic heart. Draw also from your vision, presence, and bravery as you follow the Arc of Adventure that unfolds.

> **GUIDE TIP:** Recall from basecamp that the water/empathy element addresses your basic human need to belong, to be seen and cherished as whole, perfectly imperfect, and complete as you are. It taps into heart energy and the natural desire for genuine, compassionate connections within yourself and among those around you. Use it to engage in deep listening and to intuit when, where, why, and how to offer and request acts of kindness, love, and intimacy.

> Remember, all disruptions "excite" your emotions. Their job is to rouse a response and get you moving forward. Allowing space to connect with feelings is a necessary ingredient in all adventures. Without the flow of emotion, there is no movement, only stagnation.

Explore the deeper meaning of the water/empathy power element.

- Trace the etymology of words like water, heart, love, emotion, and empathy. What resonates beyond your initial definitions? What other words compel you to discover more? What common concepts keep showing up?

- Where might you find metaphorical, symbolic, or mythical representation across time periods, cultures, and art forms? If you had to design your own symbol for this power element, what would it entail? A heart? The masks of comedy and tragedy? Two hands interlocked?

- Research the practices used around the world to generate greater empathy and rejuvenate heart power by implementing:

  Deep listening and emotional affirmation practices—within yourself first, then reflecting back with another.

  Nonverbal communication through eye contact, body mirroring, and permission-based touch.

  Live storytelling—hosting events and gatherings, sharing the human condition—with family, friends, strangers, and communities.

  Expression of emotional energy and the human condition through visual arts, mime, music, theatre, poetry, architecture, and other forms.

- Start drafting your list of possible heart adventures. Which ones are calling to the compassionate humanitarian in you?

Conduct an audit: where in your life is empathy over- or under-represented?

- Test this by asking, "What emotional current is most active in me and around me?"
- On a piece of paper, take note of the many levels of emotional current alive inside you—the sensations, sentiments, and stories in your heart. For example:

If your page is overflowing, what themes seem to be most prevalent? How would you convey these without words, perhaps in a sound, facial expression, or physical gesture?

If you don't get an immediate answer, start by naming any single emotion. Follow that with several rounds of "Why is that feeling important?" and "And why is *that* feeling important?" until you to get to the heart of your current emotional storyline.

- Overall, how much of your emotional activity is purely surface level? Do you feel numb or blocked from dipping into the current running beneath? Are your emotions trickling along like a babbling brook, about to swell like a rogue wave, or are they spilling over everyone and everything in their path like a torrential downpour?

Expand your emotional vocabulary to foster heartfelt connections.

- Research the primary and secondary emotions. Gather lists and emotion wheels from a few sources. Practice expressing genuine sentiment, beyond surface level, throw-away descriptors like "interested," "excited," "stressed," or "meh."

- Explore how and where emotions are processed in your brain, then how they are stored and released (or trapped) in your body. How have different cultures used body maps to understand, track, and heal the flow of energy fields? Which of these have stood the test of time? Which is modern society finding its way back to?

- Get creative with the properties of specific emotions (pick three in your current mix to play with). What size and shape are your selected emotions? What would each feel like to touch? What would each taste like? What kind of sound does each make? What nicknames would you give them? If they had voices, what would each say?

- Which nonverbal cues are clear signals of emotional expression? How do the best poker players, trial lawyers, chess masters, and magicians use nonverbal cues and tells to read the room, gain advantage, or set up audiences for the final act? How do emotions help to gauge incentives and motivations, especially when what people say is incongruent with how they behave or when intention is out of sync with impact?

- What do you want to borrow from and build into your own toolkit?

It's go time! Your heart adventures await!

- Which of your discoveries feel intriguing, worth pursuing, and most calling to the adventurer in you? Does how you feel now resonate with any other times from your past?

- What symbol, totem, or type of energy best represents your holistic heart then and now?

- How will you draw from that to fuel more emotional growth in your life today?

- Define what psychological safety means to you. How might that look different based on culture, gender, age, or other variables? What are the key ingredients to setting up such a space for yourself and for others?

- Commit to a simple and regular emotional tune-in practice—upon waking or before sleeping, when preparing for a conversation or before responding to a comment, and at the start or end of a group meeting or team huddle.

- Try inviting a single word or sentiment that best captures how you feel physically, mentally, emotionally, and spiritually (or sexually)…or a single word or sentiment that accurately captures the current mood in your body, in your heart, in your head, in your soul.

- What are your key boundaries for inviting or accepting emotional honesty? How would you approach and apply these differently when alone versus with others, in professional versus personal situations, with a parent or child, and while on an electrifying date or in a long-term partnership?

- Once an emotional current has been opened, how would you go about developing or enlarging it? How might you express the deepest emotional voice inside of you? Perhaps with:

  A well-crafted piece of original writing (letter, email, post, poem, book).

  An original work of art (sketch, pastel drawing, water paint, sculpture, garden or renovation project, your own adaptation of a delicious recipe).

  Hosting an event that brings people together to enjoy passionate connections (professional conference, dinner party, virtual group experience, workshop, retreat).

  Your lifestyle choices regarding wardrobe, home décor, office design, or leisure time.

  Or…?

Set your holistic heart free to flourish and watch the world around you respond in kind.

STAGE 4:
Activate Your Capable Body

This fourth and final expedition is all about blazing new trails, acting assertively in the face of the unknown, and guarding the boundaries integral to a life worth living.

Follow the flow of activities below or use them to inspire a version of your own. Use your newfound breathing/meditation technique to revitalize your bravery and grow the power of your instinctive gut. Draw also from your vision, presence, and empathy as you follow the Arc of Adventure that unfolds.

> **GUIDE TIP:** Recall from basecamp that the fire/bravery element addresses your basic human need to live life fully, independently, and autonomously, on your own terms. It taps into primal physical energy and prepares you to blaze new trails that manifest dreams, feelings, and priorities in the physical world. Use it to release all that no longer serves your growth, to protect boundaries, to show

> strength through vulnerability, and to champion a life truly worth living.
>
> Remember, your body is simply not capable of manipulation or deceit. It holds the score of all your dreams and desires, emotional truths, and mental narratives. It is the one and only vehicle you have for bringing **all** aspects of your power to life. This expedition is as much about enjoying and challenging your physical prowess as it is about giving your body what is asks for in return.

Explore deeper meaning of the fire/bravery power element.

- Trace the etymology of words like fire, courage, vulnerability, and bravery. What resonates beyond your initial definitions? What other words compel you to discover more? What common concepts keep showing up?

- Where might you find metaphorical, symbolic, or mythical representation across time periods, cultures, and art forms? If you had to design your own symbol for this power element what would it entail? A figure on the edge of a cliff? A sailboat on a vast sea? A hand raised in triumph?

- Research the practices used around the world to generate greater bravery and rejuvenate the physical being, such as:

  Testing and challenging prior physical limits—in isolation, in nature, in competition.

  Standing firmly in the face of fear or steeling oneself to weather the storm of uncertainty.

  Stimulating sensory exhilaration or experiencing psychologically safe sexual ecstasy.

  Tending to the interplay between body chemistry and nutrition, hydration, autophagy, active recovery, and passive play to maintain physical prowess over a lifetime.

- Start drafting your list of possible physical adventures. Which ones light the fire in you?

Conduct an audit. Where in your life is bravery over- or under-represented?

- Test this by asking, "What yet unrealized and vital part of my physical being feels most worth nourishing, activating, or putting to the test?"

- Answer by using your body as a firsthand witness. Stand tall in front of a full-length mirror. Don your birthday suit for the most powerful feedback. Try out various poses that express the sort of uninhibited, virtuous, primal, or just plain badass energy you want to embody. Assume the stance of a:

    Visionary, luminary, or red-carpet celebrity.

    Thoughtful, sensory artist, writer, or poet.

    Gentle, accepting, and dependable confidante.

    Learned professor, sage, or truth seeker.

    Noble ruler of a kingdom, planet, or galaxy.

    Darkly delicious, seductive, and alluring presence.

    Risk taker, thrill seeker, or renowned explorer.

    Warrior protector of all that is kind and just.

- As you gift yourself real-time feedback, which poses reflect back to you as most comfortable and authentic? Which look flat or unconvincing? In other words:

Which physical forms feel natural and fun, like stepping into that character brings out the best in you?

Which physical forms feel awkward or distasteful, like stepping into that character just isn't possible?

- Take good notes and use them to inform which aspects of your physical prowess are most in need of some power-up adventure attention.

Do a gut check before taking the leap to follow your primal fire.

- Before rushing off, check in on the aspects of your emerging ambitions that align with revitalizing your true inner fire versus those driven by an old need to play it safe, seek validation, or assume unnecessary risk.

- As you begin to filter through adventure ideas, imagine the end game you *really* want and get comfortable with the fiery truth of the price that must be paid. Here are a few gut-check questions to get you started:

    What am I willing to leave behind? Be specific as to the comforts, routines, people, status symbols, and stuff you are committed to saying goodbye to.

What am I willing to carry forward? Be specific as to your non-negotiables, core values and convictions you'll use to endure once you leap into the unfamiliar and uncomfortable unknown.

What fear am I willing to step into? A fear of looking weak, or not so impermeable as you'd like to appear? A fear you'll lose the respect, support, or love of another? A fear of being wrong, chastised, or disregarded for never being good enough? A fear you'll be trapped in a reality you'd prefer to avoid? Or is there another deeper, darker flavor of fear that rules them all?

- If your gut-check answers make you slightly uneasy, that's a good thing. Remember you will be activating bold, forward momentum, which requires your nervous system to be fully online. It's time to push play!

- If your gut-check answers have you renegotiating the entire thing or running for the exit, pay attention. It may just be those old fears tempting you backward to that fixed, stuck, blocked place, or it may be genuinely too much at this time and appropriate to start with a smaller dose.

- Either way, keep the direction of your fire pointed toward the type of power your physical being is really asking for.

It's go time! Your body adventures await!

- Which of your discoveries feel intriguing, worth pursuing, and most calling to the adventurer in you? Does how you feel now resonate with any other times from your past?

- What symbol, totem, or type of energy best represents gut instinct then and now? How will you draw from that to fuel more physical prowess in your life today?

- What daring, audacious, fun, and fearless challenges are calling to you? Perhaps a:

  Holistic medical work-up, nutritional cleanse, or daily-routine restart.

  Form of passionate athletic and artistic expression (Latin dance, Aikido, yoga).

  Pilgrimage trek through a jungle or mountain range or across a desert or ocean.

  Sensory or sexual experience that would feel wild, delicious, and soul nourishing.

  Challenge that excites your sense of danger and vulnerability (open-water swimming, entering the company of wild creatures in their natural habitats, rock climbing).

Step into the fire that burns away clutter and returns you to feeling the vitality of life coursing through your veins, living in the power of your own story, truly alive.

> **CONCLUSION:**
>
> **Your Rite of Passage**

Congratulations! You've completed each expedition on the Power Adventure to revitalize your potency. You've grown the best of who you are and have earned the right to say:

🚩 *I embody agile and effortless power. I celebrate the sanctity of life and respect the impermanence in all things by:*

- ☑ Unleashing the power of my irrepressible spirit
    (my innate vision)

- ☑ Stimulating the power of my magnificent mind
    (my innate presence)

- ☑ Expanding the power of my holistic heart
    (my innate empathy)

- ☑ Activating the power of my capable body
    (my innate bravery)

💡 **GUIDE TIP:** If these personal testaments don't yet ring true, be honest. Your tank is fuller than it was, but you haven't yet reached the fullness of power within you. Enjoy the ride; there are more thrills ahead! Don't worry, you'll know when

> the next version of yourself is ready to be redefined...then it's back to the Freedom Adventure!

Celebrate the milestone!

As the Power Adventure is akin to renewal, give some thought on how to symbolize the vitality flowing effortlessly in you, around you, and through you. Here are some ideas to get you started.

- Create a multi-day solo experience that allows you to close out one chapter and open another with grace and dignity. Consider the ceremonial role of fire and water—literal or metaphorical—in marking natural endings, healing old wounds, setting past stories adrift, and beginning again. Refresh and rejuvenate new commitments at your new power altitude and attitude.

- Go on a pilgrimage or find a place of significant meaning. Keep space in your thoughts to acknowledge those who played a vital role in your renewal—for better or worse, either as direct catalyst or by patiently and lovingly giving you space.

- After completion, pass it on. Be a spark to ignite powerful transformation in *others* by sharing your story—on stage, by video, in writing, or in quiet conversation.

Some examples of power rites of passage from my own playbook include:

- From high on rocky cliffs, driving a special logo-marked golf ball into the Atlantic ocean from the 18th hole in a private ceremony to honor the passing of one family story into another yet to be written.

- Using each minute of race day of a 140.6 mile triathlon to commemorate and give thanks for the countless spirit, mind, heart, and body challenges that liberated my transition into an exciting new life chapter.

- Engaging in a guided sacred medicine ceremony to explore how best to channel my revitalized power into new work, romance, and athletic adventures. Riding the waves of hopes, fears, and expectations. Rising to embrace the answers received.

❖ ❖ ❖

PART 3

WELCOME BACK TO BASECAMP!

Toss your bags. Grab a coffee. Find a chair. Rejoin the circle.

Everything is familiar…and yet, something is different. You can't quite put your finger on it. You're more at ease in the same surroundings. More clear and confident. More solid and secure. More at home.

Trust that. You've earned it.

Think back to all those disruptions and stirred-up emotions. The countless ways your mind grasped for meaning. Those whispers of fear—frustration, envy, avoidance, rumination—creating fictional stories that serve only to hijack your adventure path.

You chose instead to trust in yourself in the uncertain and unknown. You arrived to find payoffs and prizes meant just for you. Breakthroughs and epiphanies. Soulful sadness, tears of understanding, and relief. Love, laughter, and lightness. Joy and bliss. All the rest of it, beyond anything you imagined.

New levels of freedom, courage, and power are now part of you. You see the world, your place and time in it, from a whole new altitude. You've adopted a whole new attitude and have everything required to enjoy a life of adventure.

> *The greatest tragedy following any adventure is to have had the experience but missed the meaning.*

Children are permitted the innocent gift of hope. Adventurers know that hope alone isn't enough. We know where we've come from and where we're going. We own each step forward, even when we do not know the way. We aren't satisfied with wishful thinking. We want the kind of growth that lasts and transforms.

It is how we *react* to our adventures that makes all the difference. Which is why at the end of every adventure, before we reengage with the world waiting for us, we commit to reflecting on all we've experienced and integrating what we've learned.

Whether you've arrived back at basecamp after trying a few expeditions, finishing one of the three adventures, or completing the entire Freedom-Courage-Power Adventure circuit, our final work together is to assimilate your experiences into the life you're returning to in meaningful and lasting ways.

In the pages ahead, you'll learn how to *react* following each adventure, a simple process to extract real meaning and maximize transformational growth. I'll also guide you on how to reenter your life and traverse the most common post-adventure pitfalls. We'll finish with a final recap and leave you with everything you'll ever need to succeed in a life of adventure.

CHAPTER 7

How to Extract Real Meaning and Ensure Lasting Growth

For centuries, the best military leaders have finished each mission with a formal operational debrief, or "after action review." In other fields, those organizations, teams, and individuals equally committed to lasting growth make use of the "post mortem," another form of comprehensive and objective review following any death or ending, literal or metaphorical. Examples are:

- A medical practitioner or surgical team following a challenging procedure.

- A sports club or athlete before moving on to the next game, series, or season.

- A professional executive team or board of directors after completing a critical project.

- A parent, couple, or family after navigating a defining moment.

These types of debriefs add value, whatever the situation—whether the outcome was deemed a towering success, catastrophic failure, or somewhere between. One's potential for transformational growth is contingent upon commitment to a deliberate learning process.

Which situations from your life leave you wanting a second chance? Another try? A complete do-over?

The RE-ACT (Reflection, Evaluation, Attribution, Contribution, Transition) process is the approach I encourage following each and every adventure. After landing or losing the big deal. After a blowup or breakthrough conversation. With the team in the boardroom. At halftime in the locker room. Upon reaching that big milestone.

Imagine having the magical ability to push the pause button and rewind to any scene from your past. You can go back to what happened yesterday, last Tuesday, or five years ago. As you freeze-frame that moment, you get to:

- RE-turn to that critical moment of truth.

- RE-frame your perspective and approach.

- RE-play your moves.

CHAPTER 7: EXTRACT REAL MEANING   309

Only this time, you're blessed with the kind of 20/20 hindsight, insight, and foresight that wasn't available the first time around. This time you're able to call upon your *real* freedom, courage, and power. This time you're able to draw from *more* wisdom, *more* compassion, *more* creativity, *more* confidence.

That's what I mean by RE-ACT: literally gifting yourself (and others) a re-do on how you'd act differently a second time around with the experience-based learning available today.

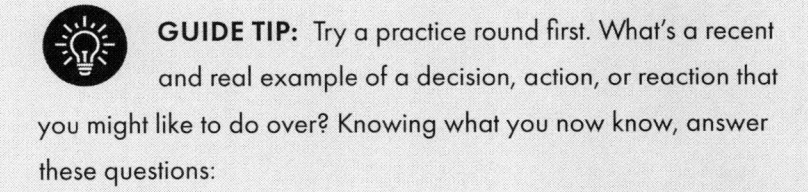

> **GUIDE TIP:** Try a practice round first. What's a recent and real example of a decision, action, or reaction that you might like to do over? Knowing what you now know, answer these questions:
>
> - What would you choose to think, or not think?
>
> - How would that leave you feeling, or not feeling?
>
> - What might that lead you to say, or not say? Do, or not do?
>
> - How might the rest of the scene play out differently as a result?

EXTRACTING LASTING VALUE FROM YOUR ADVENTURE

The RE-ACT process guides you through five open-ended questions. With practice, you'll be able to realize transformational growth from adventures big and small throughout your day-to-day life. (Note: this process works equally well when mentoring or coaching others to find the real meaning in their own experiences.)

1. Reflection: What did you intend to happen? (Or imagine would happen?)

The first step is to return to where you started. Reassert your initial hypothesis and anticipated outcome:

- What was your initial assessment of the situation?
- Did you see it as a problem to fix? An opportunity to explore?
- How did all of that leave you feeling?
- What assumptions did you make?
- What options did you consider?
- What actions did you decide upon?
- What expectations did you hold?

GUIDE TIP: Being thorough in this first step is important. For best results, adopt a reflective outlook, by expanding the full etymology of the word. "Reflective" means to:

- Go back to the place of origin.

- Hold your initial assumptions and beliefs as flexible.

- Throw light from all vantage points; illuminate all dark places.

- See all of what transpired, with reverence, grace, and humility.

2. Evaluation: What actually happened?

The next step is to unearth the few, essential, and indisputable facts that tell the real story of what transpired. You'll likely need to sift through a variety of perspectives and interpretations, starting with your own.

GUIDE TIP: Like a detective with an intuitive instinct to seek undeniable evidence, you'll need to remain independent and detached in order to arrive at an objective reality. Remember, all are entitled to their own opinions, but the facts speak for themselves.

3. Attribution: Why did that happen, in that way?

This is where you start to piece together correlations and natural consequences. Frame an unbiased assessment of what actually happened to highlight the size of gap between initial intention and actual impact, both immediate and downstream.

> **GUIDE TIP:** Maintain that impartial stance to capture the factors and variables in and out of your control. Be mindful not to over-identify with success or failure. See the forces at work beyond you and your expectations.

4. Contribution: What was my role?

Time to take an honest look in the mirror and see *yourself* as an active variable in the mix. No doubt a few key actions you took led to positive results, which you'll want to log and draw from in the future. But don't forget to also delve into:

- Actions you *could have* been taken but avoided, and to what end. Probe into your underlying motivation. *Why* did you prevent, shun, or sidestep those actions? What story, belief, or incentive was served?

- Actions that *were* taken to manipulate, coerce, or control people and situations *outside of your control*, and to what end. Again, be sure to probe into the *why* of those actions.

> **GUIDE TIP:** Once again, it's time to set your ego aside or risk recasting the true meaning of your experience into one of those worn-out, fictional storylines.

> The helpless victim. The evil villain to blame for everything. The hero required to swoop in and make everything right again. Be on the lookout for the classic blame game; don't play accountability hot potato.

5. Transition: To what action(s) am I now willing to commit?

The final step is about unlocking lasting, transformational growth versus the kind of change that lacks traction or backslides altogether. It is the litmus test for how you'll treat this new lease on life, this time from a higher altitude, equipped with a more enlightened attitude. Ask yourself the questions:

- What do I want now?
- Why is that so important to me?
- What am I willing to leave behind?
- What will I carry forward?
- What is my next big adventure?

Honest and succinct answers to those questions will upgrade a reconstituted version of who you've become post-adventure and clear intuition to map your way forward.

> **GUIDE TIP:** Again, this is another important step to be thorough with. For best results, adopt an integrative approach, by expanding the full etymology of the word. The origins of the word "integrate" are:
>
> - Integer, *integratus, intregrare*—meaning to bring distinct parts together; to render whole, and complete again.
> - *Integratio*—meaning renewal, restoration; rebirth.

Consider your post-adventure reactions an ethical duty to construct a more meaningful picture of who you are becoming. This moment is *the* opportunity to confront what you are now ready, willing, and able to change for the better, and never look back.

* * *

FINAL TIPS FOR GETTING THE MOST OUT OF HOW YOU RE-ACT

Be sure to go through the RE-ACT process while the pertinent facts, emotional currents, mental interpretations, and resulting actions and impacts are easy to accurately access (e.g., within the first few days or week). You'll thank yourself for keeping a journal or adventure logbook, as real-time notes taken along the way will support your recall of events big and small. (Hint: It's within the small, seemingly innocuous details where the most meaning often lies.)

Whether you're going through this process on your own, as part of a team, or in a relationship (couples and families), you'll get the best learning if all participants do their work first, individually, before inviting and sharing honest inputs from others. We're all drawn to our own versions of "the truth," even when debriefing the same shared experience. That's okay, as long as the bias that once fogged your view gets wiped away, leaving an honest mirror to clearly reflect back inputs and insights from all angles.

Throughout each step, stay open, patient, and deliberate. Keep your frequency tuned in to the big questions instead of rushing to fill in all the blanks. If the answer doesn't come immediately, let silence do the work and trust the information you need will present itself in time. You never know when or where a salient epiphany will arise in the days, weeks, months, and even years after an adventure.

CHAPTER 8

How to Traverse the Most Common Post-Adventure Pitfalls

Most of us return to our lives post-adventure keen to unleash the upgraded versions of ourselves and everything we've learned onto the entire world. But both you and your world will benefit from taking time to adjust. Rushing will result in frustration, and before long, your biggest adventure takeaways will fade into distant memory.

Said another way, if upon returning home, your plan for Day 1 looks anything like this, beware!

- *Wake at 4:00 a.m. for one-hour meditation followed by free-flow writing*

- *Empty all cupboards; start all-organic, all-vegan diet; cut caffeine, sugar, processed food*

- *Implement a two-hour work day; double revenue and change culture in first thirty days*

- *Lunchtime—forty-five-minute high-intensity CrossFit and forty-five-minute hot yoga warm-down*

- *Afternoons—start guitar lessons, become fluent in Spanish, and read more fiction*

- *Implement 5:00 p.m. "screens away" family policy*

- *Wind down by 7:00 p.m., dim lights, and sip Calea Zacatechichi tea in a hot bath*

- *Lead partner through tantric sexual practice*

- *Lights out and asleep by 9:15 p.m.*

- *Repeat*

Slow down, fellow adventurer. Your reentry into the life you left behind is best done as a gradual process in measured doses. Be sure to schedule transition time for yourself—on route or in the first few days—to develop your own integration approach that is realistic and achievable given the forces around you. Building simple, easy, impossible-to-negotiate-with steps is key. You can always add once your momentum gets rolling.

To get you started, here are five of the most common post-adventure pitfalls you can anticipate and a few tips on how to avoid them.

PITFALL #1: SHARING TOO MUCH, TOO OFTEN

You return bursting to tell everyone (and anyone) each little detail of your adventure. Sure, people will listen because they love and support you. But they're not going to understand the depth and nuance of your experience. And that's okay.

Re-entry tip: Know the adventure was yours alone.

It's normal for people to be curious and maybe a bit envious. Develop a headline-level summary of your primary adventure hypothesis and takeaway to share ("My initial intention was…" or "What I came to discover was…") but resist walking everyone through the play-by-play. Just *be* the person you are now, without all the back story and explanations.

Live by the Latin code "esta non verba"—
deeds, not words.

Remember, before embarking on your adventure, you spent years, maybe decades, training people to see you and experience you in a certain way. Now your job is to retrain them to trust you in a whole new way. Your grand resolutions and bold intentions carry no weight. The only real difference maker will come through your demonstrated behavior, patterned consistently, and its impact, which others will learn to rely on. That will take some time.

The more you stick with it, the more they'll notice and come to believe in the difference.

PITFALL #2: FORCING YOUR LEARNING ON OTHERS (ESPECIALLY THOSE CLOSEST TO YOU)

Yes, from this new altitude and attitude, you'll start to see the triumphs and plight of others in a whole new way.

No, your adventure experience is not the quintessential teaching moment for the rest of the world. You weren't suddenly crowned supreme elder, coach, and counselor to the masses. That mindset will only alienate loved ones and friends, while you get frustrated when people just don't "get it."

Re-entry tip: Stay in your lane.

Remember the importance of gifting everyone the dignity of their own choices. Honor their lives as their own and trust in the meaningful breakdowns and breakthroughs that await in their own adventures.

Recall that leading oneself is both challenge and adventure enough. Your only job is to live by your newfound freedom, courage, and power.

PITFALL #3: TACKLING TOO MANY IDEAS AND COMMITMENTS ALL AT ONCE

Attention, type As and consummate overachievers: you *know* this is coming.

The familiar drive to take on more. The extreme lens of "right or wrong, all or nothing." The pull to pile on more shiny new goals before first ending those habits, beliefs, or relationships that only serve to block your ability to experience *lasting* change.

As the saying goes: if everything is a priority, nothing is a priority.

Re-entry tip: Invest in progress, not pefrection. *(See, making mistakes isn't so hard.)*

Start by picking one or two simple things to *stop* doing. Mark your progress and celebrate small wins. The pattern of saying no will soon have you building the right momentum to say yes to the open space you've created.

Then proceed slowly with what you introduce. Pick forward moves that are 100 percent in your control. Err on the side of a smaller dose than what you think possible, so as to leave no room for last-minute negotiation or compromise. Consider, for example:

- Introducing to your day a five-minute practice of breathing, meditation, stretching, or core work.

- Downloading a new podcast. Try taking physical, handwritten notes in a notebook dedicated to a new learning topic.

- Investing a weekend afternoon to a new creative outlet, like writing, gardening, bird watching, trying a new recipe, or making music.

- Keeping a sketchpad handy for illustrating early-stage concepts or jotting down fun ideas, epiphanies, and dreams while they're still fresh.

- Rising early and committing to first getting fresh air, taking a light walk, or interacting with animals or nature before refueling with high-octane hydration and nutrition.

Hint: Start by committing small today, then small again tomorrow, and renew further commitment after that. Don't forget to celebrate each and every new beginning. Before long, the small wins will snowball into the sort of transformation growth you were meant to realize.

PITFALL #4: ASKING OTHERS FOR ADVICE OR ASKING THEM TO POLICE YOUR PROGRESS

This is another familiar favorite, which now you recognize as an attempt to duck the genuine work of adventure and skip straight to the prize table.

The whole point of your new adventure orientation is to get more and more practiced moving into uncertainty and living beyond fear. To become even more agile and adept at navigating messy emotions and fixed mental meanings. To maximize your time in the thrills that follow. Asking someone else to do the work for you is like calling up the understudy on opening night of your own starring role.

> *Accountability is not really something you can outsource (try as you might). Ask yourself honestly: why would you want to?*

And be mindful not to confuse the real jobs of those closest to you. Your friend is not your coach. Your partner is not your therapist. Your kids are not your pupils. You are responsible for your own life of adventure: act like it.

Re-entry tip: Befriend and engage other adventurers to your inner circle.

As you reorient your life, make time to seek out other adventurers. You know how to spot them, as they do you. Real adventurers trade on lived experience and rarely give advice. They don't fall for the "please hold me accountable" game and know exactly how to honor your journey by providing the actual support you'll benefit from most.

Engage those who come with their own adventure stories and scars. Those who believe in you and your life of adventure. Join a special interest group or club. Hire a qualified coach, therapist, trainer, or other subject-matter expert who will keep the accountability ball in *your* court, while maintaining the objectivity to say what you're most in need of hearing.

As you invest in support relationships old and new, consider the sorts of characters best positioned to keep you living free, courageous, and powerful. Find those who will call you on your own bullshit or spot you heading down another detour.

It's often said that our general dispositions and outlooks on life are dramatically affected by the five people we spend most of our time with. The energy they give off, for better or for worse, is highly contagious. That's worth paying attention to.

> *Count on one hand the five people you spend the most time with? How well does that mix of people support your life of adventure?*

As you determine how best to declutter, build, and rebuild your inner circle, start with the four elements of your divine design and their essential characteristics. You'll want four of your relationships to represent the four different elements. Look for:

- An uplifting cheerleader, whose resilience and limitless sense of vision and possibility helps keep your sights set skyward and your creative juices flowing.

- A wise mentor, whose sage-like counsel helps you stay present and grounded with what's most real and focused on what matters most.

- A gifted listener, whose calm and empathetic presence helps mirror back your emotional frequency and helps you stay tuned in to matters of the heart.

- A clever contrarian, or inspirational badass, whose fiery confidence pushes your limits and challenges you to discover and follow the path that has you feeling most alive.

With one of each of those types in your inner circle, you still have room for one more. Given what you know about yourself, where you most want to go, and what you most need to get there, if you had to double-down on one type, which would best serve you?

And this is the perfect time to explore what type of support you offer others in return. (Hint: Start by asking what others value most in you and how that aligns to their most important priorities at this time.)

PITFALL #5: EXPECTING A JOYOUS RECEPTION AND AN IMMEDIATE END TO ALL YOUR PROBLEMS

Just because you've returned with newfound freedom, courage, and power doesn't mean the rest of the world will roll out the red carpet. The people closest to you may be cautious, skeptical, or blatantly refuse to accept your reoriented way of being.

It's very possible that this newly upgraded version of who you've become will trigger their own unresolved issues. You can expect to surface those same fears you've come to know so much about: frustration, envy, anxiety, and regret. Your adventure may well be the catalyst for further tension.

If that's the case, another relationship adventure may be about to begin. This time, you'll be ready.

Re-entry tip: Embrace disruption as the start of your next adventure.

An adventurous life comes with new challenges, by definition.

No doubt, old tensions will be waiting for you, right where you left them. Instead of resisting, rise to them. Harness those feelings of unresolved conflict, frustration, and anger, to *fuel* your resolve. Those signals point to the parts of your life that you have enabled in some way and no longer want to tolerate. Now equipped with the right adventure altitude and attitude, you have the wherewithal to pursue the change you most want.

From now on you are authentically independent, able to thrive in relationships of collective prosperity, effortlessly vital in your use of vision, empathy, presence, and bravery.

From now on, each and every problem you encounter can be recast as the trailhead of yet another adventure. It's your choice whether to pick up the trail or stay poised for the next adventure call more deserving of your time and energy.

Return Home

Settled in, replaying highlights.
A bountiful day of life, love, work, and play.

The stretch of shadows.
Must be around 9:00 p.m.—perfect.

All told, a natural ending. Another clean pass.
Strong, calm, and slowed breathing, as I turn the page
                                                    all
                                                              over
                                                                       again…

Sigh...
welcome restorative sleep,
drifting blissful and open
into the marvels of subconscious sight

Standing tall, **breathing** panoramas of mountain and meadow
Sunlit glitter **dancing** on glacial lakes
Strong winds **touch** treetops at altitude
Mesmerized in **awe** by the gravity

and MAJESTY of it ALL...

how did I get here?
where is *here*...Blackcomb? Breckenridge? or...?

no matter when enchanted by subtle significances and timeless truths
as if designed just for me

alone and attuned...the smell of smoke...a crackle of fire
a magic zip line appears. Beyond fear I am:

Mentally: SHARP
Emotionally: VIBRANT
Physically: AGILE
Spiritually: RADIANT

hands steady, zipping downward, building speed...buzzing spark of metal
on metal...broken cable ahead...sensory surge!

distant scene emerging... lakefront cabin...familiar faces crowded on the dock...
all shapes, sizes, colors...smiling, laughing, clapping in encouragement...

"but wait! what if...?"

A quiet knowing, as suddenly I realize for myself a fresh breeze rising up...

a gentle whisper...a soulful invitation
to lay down the great burden...

and I let go

Miraculous freshwater plunge, immersed, silent, weightless,
instinctual swim...up and out...pulled into a circle of warm embrace.

Cut to fade...

Stirred to wake. 2:11 a.m.

Scribble notes in bedside journal.

Then back to sleep, my boy.

More adventure awaits.

CHAPTER 9

In Retrospect, It Was All One Big Adventure

ON THE OUTSIDE, IT ALL LOOKED GOOD. INSIDE, IT WAS A CELEbration for the ages.

News flash: your adventures are never done.

You are a dynamic, continually evolving being. You were not designed to ever be "done." There is no finish line. No final trophy that will make everything okay. No net worth dollar amount that proves you've finally made it. Growing up is what adventure is all about, from your first breath until your last.

Expect to be tested. Continually. Your adventures with freedom, courage, and power act like a never-ending circuit. Each lap you take is brilliantly conceived, according to your precise specifications, in whatever your present condition, to guide your rise back to the altitude and attitude from which you were designed to live.

Choosing a lifetime of adventure comes with infinite reward: everything you need, in any given moment, equipping you for whatever comes next. The right lessons will arrive at just the right times, inviting the best of your nature to come forward.

Through adventure, we develop comfort and familiarity with risk, uncertainty, and volatility. We may even welcome it as the gateway to expand into the next big versions of ourselves. The more we see our old childhood patterns, the more we can own our adult choices. Adventure eventually becomes second nature to how we explore options and make decisions that shape the trajectory of our lives—that shape our relationship to work, money, friendships, intimacy, and sex.

At any age and stage, that core hardwiring informs us of what it means to be a leader, follower, parent, spouse, employee, coworker, romantic partner, best friend, citizen, taxpayer, and student of life. Put it all together and you can see how adventure literally lives inside us, from our first steps to our last.

In the end, we are defined only by that which we move beyond.

Your time is now.

SUCCEEDING IN A LIFETIME OF ADVENTURE

Fellow adventurer, you have traveled far, conquered much, and returned anew.

Until we meet again, my final contribution to your success in choosing a life of adventure is offered in three parts:

- **Clean Pass.** The poem at the beginning of this book I wrote in appreciation for generations of ancestral adventurers whose triumphs and failings paved the way for me to create, experience, and grow through my own; and to all those who follow, may you find the vision, presence, empathy, and bravery to light your way until it comes time to pass the torch.

- **Adventurer's Creed.** The set of agreements in the next section can be used as part of a daily solo centering exercise or to align a collective around common norms. I use versions of it personally and when leading small-group or team adventure programs and large audience seminars.

- **My Personal Adventure Checklist.** The headlines and key takeaways from each major portion of our journey through the three greatest adventures. They have been transcribed in first person so you can approach or adopt them as your own.

Consider these parts of your new toolkit to commemorate and ritualize your adventure experiences. If they work for you, take a photo. Create a screensaver. Put a copy on your desk or on your fridge. Enter a version at the front of your journal. (Hint: Seeing and reading them in your own handwriting is more effective.)

Share them with someone close to you or with a complete stranger.

Or, create your own, better version, custom-suited to your life of adventure. If you do, flip me a copy so I can pass it along, with full credit and acknowledgment.

I trust our paths will pass again.

Until then, adventure on.

—MJB

Adventurer's Creed

On this day I am here to adventure. To stake claim to the altitude and attitude from which I was designed to live.

I follow the Arc of Adventure, beginning with each spark of disruption. From the mess of emotional excitement and the mental grasp to fix meaning, I choose to move forward into the unknown and toward the prize waiting beyond.

I am made for this. Everything I need has been preloaded into my divine design:

- I have the vision to imagine inspiring possibilities.

- I have the empathy to feel compassionate connections within myself and others.

- I have the presence to stay grounded with what is most real and worthy of my best and complete attention.

- I have the bravery to blaze new trails in pursuit of a life truly worth living.

On the Freedom Adventure, I rise to discover my authentic independence.

On the Courage Adventure, I rise to create collective prosperity.

On the Power Adventure, I rise to embody a vital life.

After each adventure, I make real time to extract personal meaning, ignite my growth, and recommit to my role in manifesting the life I want most.

I am here to adventure. To stake claim to the altitude and attitude from which I was designed to live.

_____   _____   _____
My Name   Today's Date   Witness

My Personal Adventure Checklist

BASECAMP CHECKLIST

Orientation Part 1: the Anatomy of Adventure. Commercial stereotypes robbed me of the truth of adventure; I'm stealing it back.

"To adventure" means choosing to see each new disruption as a personally fortuitous moment—my invitation to grow beyond and into unknown thrills waiting ahead.

The truths of adventure:

- ☑ Adventure surrounds me. Always. Patiently, persistently inviting me in, through and beyond.

- ☑ Adventure is about discovering what's most worth living for, right here, right now, and can be simple and straightforward.

- ☑ Adventure is about living at my own continually expanding edge while respecting physical and psychological safety.

- ☑ Adventure starts when discomfort kicks in.
- ☑ Adventure begins with a solo intention.

Orientation Part 2: the Arc of Adventure. Every adventure follows a predictable path:

The Spark: The ground zero of every adventure. When disruptive change comes calling, small or significant, by random chance or intentional design.

The Mess: When prior balance is disturbed, order is set adrift. My sense of normal becomes unhinged. As uncertainty rules, my emotions get excited and exposed.

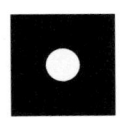

The Fix: The mental grasp for meaning. My attempt to restore order and regain control. To protect what feels emotionally exposed, at all costs.

The Choice: The incarnation of agency. My option to either remain fixed by fear in a past that is no more or to trust my ability to move beyond fear and into the unknown.

The Prize: A return to balance. Celebrating my birth into a new and complete "whole." Centered in authentic and effortless connection with forces around me and beyond me. My life at its most brilliant.

Orientation Part 3: the Axes of Adventure. My divine design comes preloaded with the four essentials elements required for a lifetime of adventure:

> **Vision:** my innate ability to look up, dream, and imagine inspiring possibilities "outside-the-box" from any reality I've experienced so far.

> **Presence:** my innate ability to stay grounded with reality, to focus on the facts, questions, and decisions most worthy of my best and complete attention.

Together when paired on a vertical axis, vision and presence represent my adventure **altitude**, which I use to maintain line of sight between future possibility and current reality:

> **Empathy:** my innate ability to feel the flow of kind and compassionate connections within myself, with others, and the world around me.

> **Bravery:** my innate ability to blaze new trails, take assertive action in the face of the unknown, and guard the boundaries integral to my life of noble purpose.

Together when paired on a horizontal axis, empathy and bravery represent my adventure **attitude**, which I use to amplify the impact of both loving kindness and risk taking.

FREEDOM ADVENTURE CHECKLIST

The path to authentic independence. Knowing myself fully requires me to:

- ☑ Derive new meaning from my past (to emerge complete)
- ☑ Master my strengths and fears (to emerge capable)
- ☑ Trust my mantra in life, breath to bone (to emerge clear)

🚩 **Rite of Passage:** I belong to this moment, and it to me. I am complete, capable, and clear, and ready to join forces with the world.

COURAGE ADVENTURE CHECKLIST

The path to collective prosperity. Showing myself fully requires me to:

- ☑ See and savor the essence of life around me (beyond my old projections)
- ☑ Accept and acknowledge differences (releasing any need to control)
- ☑ Choose how best to thrive in the world of relationships (clear with myself and clean with others)

🚩 **Rite of Passage:** Through my relationships I create prosperity beyond anything I am capable of alone. I greet the world as it is, meet others where they are, and express myself fully.

POWER ADVENTURE CHECKLIST

The path to vital renewal. Growing myself fully requires me to:

- ☑ Unleash the power of my irrepressible spirit (my innate vision)
- ☑ Stimulate the power of my magnificent mind (my innate presence)
- ☑ Expand the power of my holistic heart (my innate empathy)
- ☑ Activate the power of my capable body (my innate bravery)

🚩 **Rite of Passage:** I embody agile and effortless power. I celebrate the sanctity of life and respect the impermanence in all things.

RETURN TO BASECAMP CHECKLIST

Realizing transformational growth post-adventure depends on my ability to:

- *RE-ACT effectively by following a sequence of objective, open-ended questions:*

  What did I expect to happen? (Reflection)

  What actually happened? (Examination)

  Why did it happen, in that way? (Attribution)

  What was my role? (Contribution)

  To what path am I now willing to commit? (Transition)

- *RE-ENTER gracefully by traversing common pitfalls and remembering to:*

  Say less. Be more.

  Stay in my own lane. Leading myself is challenge and adventure enough.

  Invest in progress, not perfection. Trust the small wins to stack up.

  Befriend and engage other adventurers to my inner circle.

  Embrace disruption as the start of my next adventure.

Acknowledgments

IF, AS THE SAYING GOES, IT TAKES A VILLAGE TO RAISE A CHILD, THEN it took a metropolis to raise this book.

Heartfelt appreciation to my writing coach—award-winning and critically acclaimed author Landon J. Napoleon. Our meeting felt destined from the outset. Equal gratitude to Karen Brody, who on one fateful day in 2019 said, "Why don't you go on an adventure, and then write about it?" (a theme echoed over the years by similarly wise and insightful friends Adria Trowhill, Roger Kenrick, Mitchel Groter, and Vince Corsaro). The steady, soulful encouragement each of you provided in your own ways steered me clear from the process of writing *a* book so that I might realize the adventure of creating *this* book. Thank you.

Sarafina Riskind, and the entire team at Scribe Media, your upbeat, empathetic, and solution-minded support guided my progress through the roller-coaster ride of authorship. Tristan Stark and Jenny Shipley, your editorial challenges to say more with less were invaluable (and no doubt appreciated by all). Sarah Craig, thank you for jumping all-in with artistic collaboration on cover design and interior graphics. Jennifer Connelly, thank you, Jami Schlicher, and your spirited team as we join forces to blaze new trails for those hungry to reclaim adventure in their lives. And

Tamara Riddell, your unwavering support keeps programs running, clients happy, and me where I'm supposed to be.

I could devote hours recognizing the generations of philosophers, scientists, artists, teachers, leaders, and adventurers who have shaped my understanding of human motivations, family systems, the divine feminine and masculine, duality, and the literal and metaphorical circle of life—for a lifetime of source material that influenced this book, I am in your debt. I have done my utmost to adhere to the challenge of what T.S. Eliot would deem to be a "good poet," one who borrows from other authors "remote in time, or alien in language, or diverse in interest" to create something fresh, germane, and complete. Easier said than done, as Miles Davis reflected, "Sometimes you have to play a long time to be able to play like yourself."

I delight in sprinkling specific references and direct quotes into all my professional and day-to-day interactions, so that others may in turn find meaning, and discover how to play in *their* own way. For now, I must acknowledge and extend gratitude to the following: Joseph Campbell and *The Hero's Journey* (which for this author applies across gender); Eric Berne and Bert Hellinger (from transactional analysis to family constellations); Carl Jung (for paving the way toward understanding individuation and the collective unconscious); Elisabeth Kübler-Ross (for her seminal works on death, dying, and stages of grief); Stephen Karpman (for mapping the roles of power and conflict into "The Drama Triangle"); Karen Brody and Jim Mitchell, respectively (whose soulful coaching contributions liberate the power of the divine feminine and masculine in all of us); Melody Beattie (along with Janet Woititz and Robin Norwood, for popularizing Timmen L. Cermak's works on co-dependency, now used throughout Alcoholics Anonymous and Al-Anon); Julia Cameron (for getting me started and keeping me going through *The Artist's Way*); Siddhartha Gautama and Fayan

Weni (for their Buddhist life teachings); Roger Birkman (www.birkman.com), and Pam and Dan Boney (www.tilt365.com) for their respective creation of mass-market tools that further the appreciation of behavioral incentives, individual development, and social collaboration; David Whyte (for poetically illuminating the human condition in everyday experience); in loving memory of legendary teammate, teacher, and globetrotter Mark Alessio (whose "idle @ yes" and "graffiti story" creations live on to inspire adventure and remind us how lucky we are); and finally, to George Lucas (for the *Star Wars* universe), J.K. Rowling (for the wizarding world of *Harry Potter*), and Stephen King (for the *Dark Tower* series in particular), for their individual genius in weaving stories that keep *all* of the aforementioned works approachable and alive for generations to come.

Enormous respect and thanks to the global ecosystem of extraordinary clients, colleagues, and forum relationships with whom it has been my absolute privilege to serve, grow with, and learn from over decades—fellow adventurers all. Special thanks to my YPO and EO forum brothers and sisters who elevate the trajectory of my life. Some of these special individuals are named on this book's back cover and early pages, along with kind words that celebrate our work together. Look them up, and if by chance your paths cross, I guarantee your life will be richer for it.

Finally, my deepest gratitude goes to all members of my multifaceted family of origin, choice, and circumstance. The Boydells and Barkalows. The Connidis, Arnet, and Acres clans. The Grindstaffs, Farrells, Arces, and Abdelmessihs. All told, a vibrant cultural tapestry woven from the unique influences of the United States, Canada, England, Scotland, France, Norway, Greece, Holland, Ukraine, Spain, Egypt, and the Soudan. I want to thank each of my three parents, Craig, Ingrid, and Bonnie for their never-ending love and distinct gifts that have informed my life direction.

I am blessed with four siblings who continue to enhance my life: Patrick from the beginning; Kari through her short time with us; Kai and Nora for expanding our generational connectivity. Thanks to Eli and Maggie, for inviting me so fully into your worlds, and schooling me in the ways of female energy. To sons Troy and Jackson, I am blessed beyond measure for your presence in my life. Every day I revel in your own discovery of freedom, courage, and power in the world as men.

And to Kimberley Acres, your kind and brave heart is a brilliant beacon of light in the world. Thank you for patiently seeing and joyously celebrating all that I am. Your trust and tireless support made this book possible. The arc of our story fills my heart and fuels my soul—from tunnel of love to adventure of a lifetime, I love you all ways, always.

About the Author

MICHAEL JESS BOYDELL'S INFANT FLIGHT FROM NEW JERSEY to Hawaii arrived just in time for him to witness the Apollo 11 moon landing, foreshadowing a life of adventure—from the cloud forests of Costa Rica and corals of the Great Barrier Reef to the deeply personal, lived experience through love and loss, repair and rebirth.

Following a BA in Psychology from Queen's University and an MBA from Ivey Business School, Michael spent the first twenty years of his career rapidly ascending the ranks of corporate strategy and executive leadership with fast-paced, private and publicly held, innovation-driven multinationals, while active as a keynote speaker and board director. After orchestrating a career sabbatical, he launched an advisory practice dedicated to connecting global business leaders to their own brilliance. His contributions to Board-CEO relations, strategy and brand repositioning, and team and executive performance, continue to pave the way for transformational growth in business results, cultural health, personal fulfillment, and positive societal impact.

As an adjunct to his private practice, Michael is a former member turned globally certified facilitator with Young Presidents' Organization. Over the past decade Michael has been invited to design and lead numerous programs of deep impact with YPO's international boards and global community of YPO facilitators, along with delivering hundreds of events for regional chapters, local forums, and individual members throughout North America, Europe, and Asia.

A varsity athlete in university and graduate school, Michael went on to coach more than two dozen youth sports teams and enjoyed competing (with himself) in endurance-distance triathlon. A lifelong learner passionate about human performance, music, art, world culture, wildlife, and the great outdoors, he and his lifelong soulmate Kim are blessed with four adult children, and lead active lives of work and play wherever adventure beckons.

His first book, *The Adventure Advantage: A Roadmap Into Uncertainty, Through Fear, and Onward to Your Heroic Life* serves as a primer for those stepping into any form of important life transition. For organizations, teams, and executives ready to transform disruptive change into winning results, further solutions and programs are available including:

- *The Adventure Advantage* workbook and other self-guided tools
- In-person and virtual leadership development workshops
- Multi-day, experience-based offsites and retreats
- Podcast interviews, keynotes and professional development seminars
- In-house consulting and bespoke coaching engagements

For all this and more, visit theadventureadvantage.com or sign-up to join any one of our online adventure communities.

Manufactured by Amazon.ca
Bolton, ON